POSITIVE P

TEENAGERS
IN THE FAMILY

DEBI ROKER &
JOHN COLEMAN

OF THE TRUST FOR THE
STUDY OF ADOLESCENCE

eadway · Hodder & Stoughton

British Library Cataloguing in Publication Data

ISBN 0 340 62106 0

First published 1995
Impression number   10 9 8 7 6 5 4 3 2 1
Year   1999 1998 1997 1996 1995

Typeset by Wearset, Boldon, Tyne and Wear.
Printed in Great Britain for Hodder & Stoughton Education, a division of Hodder
Headline Plc, 338 Euston Road, London NW1 3BH by Cox & Wyman Ltd, Reading.

Contents

Trust for the Study of Adolescence

The Trust for the Study of Adolescence is an independent research and training organisation based in Brighton. It was established in 1988, and has carried out work in the areas of sexuality, divorce, teenage pregnancy and parenthood, suicide and self-harm, young offenders and adolescent altruism. The Trust has a particular interest in providing support for parents of teenagers. It has published a series of information packs in a series entitled *Tapes for Parents*. Each pack consists of a booklet and audiotape of approximately 60 minutes. Titles include:

Teenagers in the Family
Teenagers Under Stress
Teenagers and Sexuality
Teenagers and Divorce
Teenagers and Step-Parents
Teenagers and Drugs
Teenagers and Alcohol

In order to produce these packs Trust staff have interviewed a wide range of parents and teenagers. Some of the interview material from the tapes appears in this book. The Trust may be contacted at 23 New Road, Brighton, East Sussex BN1 1WZ Tel. 01273 693311, Fax 01273 679907.

Foreword

When I tell people that I thoroughly enjoyed my three children's teenage years they clearly think I'm either a liar or a masochist or a bit of both. But it's quite true. They were hard-working years, often exhausting years, certainly dreadfully expensive years, but they were never boring. Indeed, I found them fascinating. When I was small I loved watching a butterfly emerge from its chrysalis and marvelled at what had happened to my pet caterpillar. My pleasure in watching my babies turn into people was no less intense.

This book is one of the best for chrysalis nurturers I've seen. It offers parents not a finger wagging 'thou-shalt' and 'thou-shalt-not' manual on the Care and Creation of Adorable Adolescents but a clear account of the process of change that makes those babies into adults and, equally importantly, an account of the way that makes parents feel. It is poignant to see your own youth slip away as your offspring replace you as the active adults on whom the future depends. It is painful to be reminded quite so sharply of your own mortality. But it need not be depressing. You can cope with the poignancy and recover from the pain in the pleasure that comes with the successful completion of parenthood. It was what you had babies for, after all: to create new human adults. If your children never grew up, the poignancy and the pain would be infinitely greater.

As Debi Roker and John Coleman make very clear, it's essential you avoid the mind- and spirit-numbing effect of allowing other people's stereotypical notions of what it's like to live with teenagers to take root in your expectations. Being a parent of teenagers needs simply some knowledge, a good deal of common sense and above all a warm and loving heart.

In these pages you will not find the third; that you must supply yourself. But you'll find lots of the other two: not only information on the changes of puberty, but also good strategies to help you (and your teens) cope with the occasional hiccups and problems.

There's sensible advice on protecting young health and happiness (and at the same time your own!) and enormous encouragement.

This is a *smashing* book. It made me quite nostalgic for the days when my kitchen was filled with blue-jeaned bottoms, my phone was always busy with frantic calls and my fridge was constantly emptied by gannet-like adolescent appetites. Now, I find myself looking forward to being the grandmother of teenagers one day. Now, that should be interesting! We can be happily outrageous together.

Claire Rayner

CHAPTER ONE

Being a parent

> " It is easier to be a brain surgeon than a really good parent. "

These words will strike a chord with many parents of teenagers. Family life at this time can be difficult. However, the teenage years can also be an immensely enjoyable and rewarding period in a parent's life. This chapter looks at some of the ways in which adults think about and relate to young people, and at how this can influence the parent-teenager relationship. We'll look at the following:

- The generation gap
- Expectations and stereotypes of adolescence
- Understanding teenagers better
- The needs of parents

Many adults see the teenage years as puzzling or confusing. Adolescent behaviour sometimes appears contradictory, or just plain irritating. We hope this book will give you a clearer understanding of young people and their needs.

The generation gap

> ❝ They think they're right because they're older, and
> you think you're right because it's your problem
> you're talking about. ❞

As this comment from a young person demonstrates, understanding between teenagers and their parents can often be in very short supply. Adults may describe young people as obstinate, irritating, or unpredictable. To teenagers, parents may be patronising or uninterested. This discrepancy is referred to as the generation gap, and it is often presented as insurmountable. However, there are a number of steps that we can take to bridge it, many of which are discussed in this book.

The first step, perhaps, is to recognise that adolescence is a difficult time for young people. The pressures on teenagers come from all quarters. For example:

- Their bodies are changing and growing, leading to dramatic alterations in their size, shape and how they view themselves.
- There are pressures from inside the individual to experiment, to try out new identities, and to move towards more adult roles and behaviours.
- Friends, as well as advertising and TV, encourage young people to grow up at an ever-increasing rate.

Many parents feel the need to hold back their son's or daughter's move to independence, believing that they are not mature enough to cope with the real world. It is likely, of course, that the teenager too will have doubts about how fast he or she wants to grow up. Your son or daughter may well be torn between what he or she sees as the excitement and freedom of impending adulthood, and the fears and anxieties of moving away from childhood. These conflicting pressures lead to a real sense of confusion for many teenagers, which is often reflected in their behaviour. It is difficult for teenagers to know who they are. Are they children or adults? Are they dependent or independent?

Clearly, the situation is not this simple, and roles and responsibilities will change throughout the teenage years. None the less, this confusion is clearly reflected in the young person's legal status. It is perhaps inevitable that the law allows teenagers to do different things at different times. However, the result of this is an uncertainty about when any individual can be said to be adult.

It is important to put the notion of a generation gap in its proper context. The phrase implies that the generations are worlds apart. Indeed, the common view is of teenagers and parents opposed to each other in all things. There are certainly differences between parents and teenagers in some areas – for example in attitudes to sex, music, and drugs. All of the evidence available, however, suggests that this gap is not as wide as it is often presented. A variety of studies show that, in fact, there are generally positive and close relationships between parents and teenagers. The most common areas of disagreement between the two groups concern the practicalities of everday life – teenagers' appearance, the state of their bedrooms, and the time they have to be in at night.

Very few families experience constant conflict, and research shows a broad level of agreement between parents and teenagers on most fundamental values and beliefs. This is not to say, of course, that the adolescent period is problem free. The very nature of adolescence means that teenagers are testing boundaries, challenging authority, and developing their own views and ideas. There are many difficult issues for parents and teenagers to deal with – school work, sex, money, going out. But although there may well be disagreements as young people move towards adulthood, the situation rarely involves a complete breakdown of relationships.

The following section looks further at our expectations, images and stereotypes of the teenage years. Thinking about these issues is likely to help you, as a parent, develop a greater understanding of your teenager.

Expectations and stereotypes of adolescence

❝ ... there's just that assumption isn't there, that the teenage years are dreadful? ❞

This quote, from one of the parents we spoke to, summarises the general attitude of society to teenagers. 'Teenagers are difficult'. 'Teenagers are trouble'. These stereotypes will undoubtedly lead parents to have particular expectations of their children's teenage years. Many of the parents that we spoke to, including the one quoted above, said that they expected the teenage years to be extremely difficult. Some commented how friends had warned them of the 'horrors' and the 'pain' to come. For those parents who were looking back at the teenage years, however, most said that although there were periods of difficulty and anxiety, overall both they and their sons or daughters had emerged unscathed.

It is worth remembering this when faced with the prospect of a child moving into adolescence. This is not to say that particular, and potentially serious, problems will not occur; many of these areas of difficulty are discussed in later chapters of this book. But most teenagers emerge from adolescence as healthy young adults with positive relationships with their parents.

A good start to helping your family during the teenage years is to try to understand what young people are going through, to try to build good and open relationships with them, and to anticipate areas where problems might emerge. This is what we'll look at next.

Understanding teenagers better

One useful way of beginning to understand the teenage years is to remember that change is taking place in almost every area of a young person's life – their bodies, emotions, social lives, relationships, and so on. During a relatively small number of years, there is a lot for teenagers to learn and adapt to. Each young person has to come to terms with a changing body, with sexual maturity, and with new needs and feelings.

On top of all this, teenagers have to deal with the ambiguous status of young people in our society. There is no single point at which an adolescent is a grown-up – much as many teenagers would like there to be! Indeed, our society does not help young people to develop a real sense of who they are during this stage. At present, for example, a sixteen-year-old may get married but cannot get a mortgage or drive a car. He or she can join the army, but cannot vote, get tattooed, or drink alcohol in pubs. It's no wonder that young people are confused about where they stand and how they should behave.

As a result of this lack of any real status, the behaviour of teenagers can appear, and indeed often is, contradictory. It is this that can make the adolescent years so difficult. For example, a fourteen-year-old boy may one day be furious because his mother is giving him advice, and will accuse her of interfering and 'trying to run his life'. Yet the next day he may be depressed and resentful, saying that his parents show no interest in him, that they leave him to get on with things on his own, and 'don't seem to care what happens...' This sort of contradictory behaviour leaves many parents at a loss about what to do for the best.

Another feature of this inconsistency and unpredictability is that teenagers will often change from one mood to another very quickly. At one moment, for example, a fifteen-year-old girl can appear happy, cheerful, and full of energy, yet before you know where you are she will be slumped on her bed, looking miserable, and wanting to be left on her own. One parent described it as:

❛ ... like living with someone with multiple personalities. You never know which one she's going to be next. ❜

This sort of behaviour is, of course, very trying but it is important to try to remember that these sorts of mood swings are quite normal. They reflect all the changes happening to a young person's body, and the sense of 'up and down' that is characteristic of this stage of development.

In addition to inconsistency and unpredictability, many of the parents we spoke to pointed out that their teenagers constantly challenge them to defend and explain their views. It is infuriating to have every decision and every opinion questioned, and obviously there are times when this makes parents angry and frustrated. Teenagers often seem to go too far, being unable to accept anything – especially from their parents – without a long and drawn-out battle. Many of the parents said that this leads to a feeling of being continually on the defensive, and often results in tension within the family.

It can be extremely trying to feel you are constantly being challenged. Many parents just feel angry in response. These are difficult emotions for parents to cope with, leaving them drained and feeling guilty for things that they have said or done, especially in the heat of the moment.

It is worth trying to remind yourself at these times that adolescents have strong and angry feelings to cope with too. Teenagers often feel frustrated, as their wish to become adult almost overnight simply cannot happen. This frustration is made worse by the confusing messages given to young people by society and the law. Most importantly, perhaps, teenagers are likely to feel angry with themselves, because of their doubts, clumsiness, failures, and difficulties in making decisions and choices.

It is easy, therefore, to see how teenagers' own anger can lead to provocation of the adults around them. Young people know exactly how to wind up their parents, and can often be quite skilful in picking on issues which are guaranteed to start an argument, or to be hurtful. One parent remembered her fifteen-year-old daughter doing this consistently over the course of about a year:

BEING A PARENT

❝ *She was so good at it . . . when I'd just got in, or I was really tired. She'd find the one thing that would set us all off. It all felt so tiring and so unnecessary. I couldn't understand why she did it.* ❞

As a parent, try to remember that much of your son's or daughter's anger will have more to do with his or her own inner feelings and emotions than with your behaviour or views, and you may well feel much better about this hostility.

The way that teenagers behave often makes parents feel that they can do nothing right, and that they're not really needed. This is far from the truth. Research shows that in most families teenagers like and respect their parents, and want their support and advice as they grow up. Teenagers need to know that they are loved and valued. Parents can make a difference to their teenager's life. This book will suggest how you can play a key role in helping your teenager to become a happy and healthy young adult.

We will talk further about some of these issues in Chapter 2, including the effects of the changes of puberty on young people, and what teenagers need from their parents as they grow up. Before we do this, however, we will look at an important issue – your needs as a parent.

The needs of parents

Parents have needs too. Your life does not stop just because you have a teenager. As one of the mothers we spoke to put it when we asked about this:

❝ *I'm glad you asked about what parents need, because people often talk about what teenagers need as if their parents were robots . . . Yes, parents definitely have needs too.* ❞

So it is important to think about your needs as a parent, and how this relates to other things happening in your life. Parents of teenagers are at a particular stage in their lives. Many things will have changed since your children were born. Parents may have experienced the break-up of their marriage, become single parents, or become part of a step-family. You may be caring for your own parents or other relatives. If you have a partner, your relationship with them will have changed over the years. You may have less energy and vitality, or have health problems.

As a parent, then, you will have your own needs. It is worth reminding yourself of this throughout your child's teenage years. Teenagers need a lot of time, commitment, and effort. But you are not only a parent. You may also be a partner, or have a job. You will also have your own friends and interests. These shouldn't be abandoned just because you have teenage children. One of the fathers we spoke to described it this way:

> *I need to put my foot down sometimes, remind [my sons] that I'm not just a taxi service ready to drop everything at any time. They need to know that I've still got a life to lead too.*

There are a number of ways of approaching this, and of trying to meet your own needs as well as fulfilling your role as a parent:

- Decide what things in life (other than your children) are important to you – for example leisure activities or friends;
- Make sure your family is aware how important these other activities are to you, and that you need to make time to do them;
- Structure your time, and your family's time, to include these activities.

Being a parent of a teenager is not just about meeting the needs of teenagers. It is about both teenagers and parents developing and growing together.

In talking about the difficulties for parents we should not forget what is perhaps the most difficult issue of all – the fact that having teenagers in the family means that the principles and guidelines you developed during the childhood years have to change. These rules and principles have to be altered to meet the different demands and needs of adolescents, who will not be content to remain in a childlike position in the family.

It is never easy to change our relationships. Many parents feel a real sense of disruption, as agreements and rituals long established in the family are (often suddenly) changed. However, these changes do need to be made. If parents resist, there is likely to be an even more painful upheaval at a later point. It is a natural and inevitable stage in the lifecycle of a family and, if approached and tackled in the right way, can be quite rewarding.

Finally, it is important to remember that most parents find teenagers difficult at times. Being a parent can be an isolated and lonely experience. The guilt that is associated with challenging and difficult family relationships can be acute. But as one mother told us:

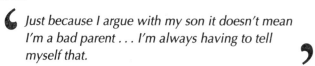

Just because I argue with my son it doesn't mean I'm a bad parent . . . I'm always having to tell myself that.

It is important not to feel that you have to cope alone. Speak to friends and family about your difficulties and worries, or contact one of the parents' organisations listed at the end of the chapter. It will also help if you understand what is happening to your teenager as they move through the adolescent years – something we discuss in the next chapter.

Useful organisations

Parentline offers help and advice to parents on all aspects of bringing up children and teenagers. Their Helpline number is 01702-559900, open 9am–6pm Monday to Friday, and 10am–2pm Saturday. There is an answerphone outside these hours. Alternatively write to: Endway House, The Endway, Hadleigh, Essex, SS7 2AN.

Exploring Parenthood offers advice, information and counselling to parents on issues of family relationships and children's development and behaviour. Their Advice Line is open 10am–4pm Monday to Friday, on 0181-9601678. There is an answerphone outside these hours. Or write to: Latimer Advice Centre, 194 Freston Road, London, W10 6TT.

CHAPTER TWO

Young people growing up

This chapter will look at the physical and sexual changes of adolescence, and at how parents can help teenagers come to terms with them. It will also look more generally at what young people need from their parents during this stage of development. The following areas will be covered:

- Physical changes during puberty
- Talking about difficult issues
- What teenagers need from their parents

Physical changes during puberty

Many changes happen to a young person's body during puberty. These changes can be confusing and worrying, so it's important that teenagers are properly prepared for what's likely to happen to them. The changes include the growth spurt, rapid changes in both height and weight, the maturation of the sexual organs, and many other alterations in the body.

The changes are of course different for boys and girls. For boys pubic and facial hair appears, the voice breaks, and the penis and testes grow in size. A boy will also experience his first wet dream at this time, becoming sexually aroused in his sleep and emitting semen. It is important that boys are prepared for this, otherwise some may feel ashamed or guilty when it happens. It is probably easier for boys to talk to a man about this, possibly their father, step-father, uncle or family friend. It will help boys to hear about how these adults felt when they were teenagers, and about their experiences of things like wet dreams.

For girls, pubic hair develops, breasts and hips grow, and periods start. Again, it is essential that a girl is prepared for this beforehand. In the next section on **Talking about difficult issues**, we suggest some ways in which parents can talk to girls about periods and the changes of puberty.

It is important to remember that there is no set pattern or sequence to the changes of puberty. The most common early sign for boys is the start of the growth spurt. For girls it is more usually the growth of pubic hair or breast development. However, changes can occur in any order.

Puberty starts at different times for boys and girls – the average age for the onset of puberty is ten to ten-and-a-half for girls, and eleven-and-a-half to twelve for boys. The changes described earlier usually take place over about two years. The difference in the timing of puberty for boys and girls explains why at this age most friendship groups are single sex.

Research shows that over the last 150 years puberty has occurred earlier and earlier. During the last 30 or 40 years in Britain, puberty has occurred approximately one month earlier for every ten years. Although the reason for this is uncertain, it is most likely to be a result of better nutrition and health care. Earlier physical and sexual maturation is, of course, going to affect how young people develop psychologically and emotionally. Certainly some young people, of whatever age, feel unprepared for the physical, sexual and psychological changes that puberty brings.

When talking about puberty, many parents ask 'what is normal?' What changes should they expect by a particular age for example? This is a very difficult question to answer, mainly because individuals vary so much. One thirteen-year-old girl, for example, may still physically be a child, with little breast development, no hips, and no pubic hair. Another may have a mature body, fully developed in all areas. Both girls are 'normal', but just at different stages of development.

Despite this, there are teenagers whom we describe as early or late developers. This is usually defined as a young person who is two to three years ahead or behind those of her or his age. Teenagers who develop early may have some advantages. For example, boys who develop strength and endurance earlier are often able to shine on the sports field. Girls who mature early are often more self-confident in their social relationships. Late developers may suffer somewhat in comparison to their peers, finding it difficult to fit in. They may feel that they are still a child, while their friends are moving into adulthood. If your teenager seems to be very late in reaching puberty it is worth remembering two things:

- that it is rare that a late developer's adjustment to adulthood is affected;
- that he or she may need extra support or encouragement in making friends and joining in with groups.

Although we usually talk about the physical changes of adolescence, it is of course important to remember that a young person is changing intellectually and emotionally as well. He or she will be developing adult intellectual skills, and will have the ability to think about a whole range of problems and issues which a year or two earlier were beyond their grasp. At an emotional level too, the young person will be experiencing many new feelings, including sexual desire.

Many parents find their son's or daughter's increasing sexuality difficult to handle, and often embarrassing. The recognition that a young person is a sexual being is important however. You may find it helps to speak to other parents who have older teenagers, to talk about their feelings and how they talked about these topics. The next section contains some practical suggestions about talking to teenagers about sexual matters.

Helping your teenager to understand what's happening

It is important that parents help young people through the changes and uncertainties of puberty.

Teenagers often have what may appear to adults to be trivial worries about their changing bodies, but which are frightening or worrying to them. These concerns need to be addressed. Helping young people through puberty can be done in a number of ways:

- Try to make discussion about the body and about sexual issues a normal part of what happens in the family; this should begin as early as possible in a child's life. If parents have talked about these issues all through their child's development – at an appropriate level of course – then discussions about the changes of puberty will be seen as just another part of this process.
- Provide materials – books, leaflets, etc. – which young people can read at home. There are many very good (and often free) publications, available from groups like the Family Planning Association, or producers of sanitary towels. Having information about the house means that teenagers can consult it as they wish. As one parent told us:

I went and bought my various books at various stages, which my children found very helpful. In fact their friends didn't know quite a lot of what was in the books, and they brought them round to look at them. We've always kept the books in the sitting room, and they are there for anybody who wants to

*look at them at any time. I don't think anyone feels
embarrassment about taking it out and reading it up.
And I've always said I'll answer any questions, or if
you've anything you want to know, I'm around.
I've left it rather to them to approach me.* **9**

This last point is important – it is often better to let young people come to you to talk about many of these things. However, it is a good idea to have made it clear that you are willing to listen and discuss issues with them beforehand.

You may, of course, still find it difficult to talk to your teenager about puberty and sex – many other parents find it difficult too! There are a number of ways that you can try to bring these topics up with your teenager. These include:

- talking about your own experience as a teenager, and your anxieties and uncertainties. This will help break down the barriers between you and your son or daughter;
- admitting that there are things that you don't know or understand about the body and how it works; it will help teenagers to realise that there are things that other people don't understand too;
- using events in TV soaps and films to start talking about issues to do with bodies and sexuality.

Talking about difficult issues

If some areas of puberty and sexuality are difficult to talk about in families, there are a number of areas which are never mentioned at all. The most common taboo subjects are menstruation, masturbation, and homosexuality. We will look at each of these briefly, and also at sex education in your teenager's school.

Menstruation

We have already said that it is essential that girls know about periods long before they occur. This will be easier for both parent and teenager if a girl's early questions about, for example, her mother's tampons or sanitary towels are answered directly and honestly. If her mother or father finds talking about this just too difficult, then someone else, maybe an aunt or a close friend, should do so. Most schools now talk to girls about periods. Ask your daughter about these lessons, and talk about things like what happens if her period starts while she's at school.

Menstruation should not, of course, be a topic only talked about by girls. Boys should also be told as much as possible about the changes to a girl's body as well as their own. This can take place when talking about the early changes of puberty. Most children and young people want to understand what's happening to them and to their friends. Build on this, and answer all the questions they have, however trivial they may seem.

Masturbation

Masturbation is another difficult area for most parents to address. It is important to understand that masturbation is no more than a way of exploring and discovering how your sexual organs work, and how they can give you pleasure. Children and teenagers should be told this. Masturbation should not be seen as a bad thing, and certainly not dirty or wrong. It is simply one form of sexual activity, a way of learning about your body.

Homosexuality

Homosexuality is a topic likely to arouse particularly strong feelings for some parents. However, a homosexual experience is a very common feature of adolescent development. It can take many forms. It may be hero worship of someone of the same sex, although it can also involve some physical exploration too.

These relationships are all part of growing up and discovering what sort of person you are. For some young people, these experiences will lead to the development of a gay or lesbian sexual orientation. We will return to this topic later, in Chapter 6.

Where parents are uncertain or worried about any aspect of their teenagers' physical or sexual development, they should seek help and advice from an appropriate organisation. Useful organisations are listed at the end of each chapter.

Sex education in schools

All secondary schools must now provide sex education for teenagers. It is normally taught as part of a course of Personal, Health and Social Education (PHSE), although it may be called different things in different schools.

Schools vary considerably in what they teach, and how. Find out what your teenager's school is and is not teaching. Ask your son or daughter what they've been learning at school, and discuss it with them. It may help too to share with them some of your own experiences and anxieties when you were their age; this is likely to make you much more approachable.

Much of the advice in this chapter is based on developing *good communication* between you and your teenager. Good communication is fundamental to understanding – and living happily with – the teenager in your family. Essential to good communication is understanding what teenagers need from their parents. It is this that we look at next.

What teenagers need from their parents

In our interviews with young people, we asked them what they thought teenagers needed from their parents. Their responses are given overleaf.

❝ Well, to know that they love you, even after you've had a row and got angry with each other. ❞

❝ I'd say to be patient, and try to remember what it's like to be my age. ❞

❝ Lots of advice and information and support . . . and to be told that they love me a lot. ❞

❝ More leeway and more understanding. They've got to have the patience to sit down and try to understand us . . . ❞

One of the needs most frequently mentioned by teenagers was for parents to have some understanding and awareness of the process of growing up. Yet, as we said in the previous chapter, parents and teenagers may well have very different views about this. Both parents and adolescents have a difficult task in negotiating a changed relationship and in recognising each other's changing needs. We have listed below some of the most important things that teenagers need from their parents. These are

- structure
- to be allowed to rebel
- time
- privacy
- to have room to grow

We will look at each of these in turn.

The need for structure

Teenagers do need structure in their lives. They need to have boundaries, and to know that there are rules. Providing structure helps teenagers to learn and internalise rules. As they take on more responsibility for their own lives, this allows them to move towards independence.

YOUNG PEOPLE GROWING UP

One of the problems for parents of teenagers is to make decisions about limits, rules, and regulations. What rules should you lay down? How should they be decided? What should you do if they are broken? How do they need to be changed as teenagers get older?

In the interviews that we had with parents and teenagers, rows and arguments in the family were often related to rules. Here's what some young people said about this:

> *What do we row about? Restrictions. When I go out my father always wishes to know, like where I am going, what times and this, that, and the other . . . You say "Oh can't I just go?" You don't want to hang around and give them all these details.*

> *We row about when I want to go out and come back late. They complain that I never think about them. And also about not doing enough housework – "You never do anything around the house" they say.*

How necessary are rules and regulations? We all need to know where we stand in our relationships, and within the groups to which we belong. All groups have rules, whether they're schools, the work-place, or families. Teenagers are no different. They need to know where they stand, and how far they can go in pushing the limits of their behaviour. Clearly, the teenage years are characterised by young people's demands for more and more freedom. As a fourteen-year-old said to us:

> *I'm not a child anymore. I want to choose my own things and live my own life. I'm nearly an adult.*

Parents have to help young people to sort out what is and what is not acceptable. They need to know that there are limits to what they can do. They need to be clear what the limits are, and they need to know what will happen if they overstep those limits.

A certain level of agreement between teenagers and their parents is essential. Otherwise it would be impossible for any family to live together under the same roof. If you have too many rules however – especially petty ones – then young people will feel that their whole lives are governed by rules and restrictions.

This means that some things must take priority. It is best to decide on a few major issues where there have to be fixed rules. Issues which affect health and personal safety would certainly fall into this category, although clearly these rules will change as teenagers get older. You might insist, for example, that a twelve-year-old is picked up from a friends house at 7pm; a sixteen-year-old might be allowed to get the bus home at a later time. As one father explained to us:

> ... the fourteen-year-old, she's obviously monitored and well ... managed. The seventeen-year-old, well, she really manages herself. But we keep an eye open for the important things of course.

In our interviews with parents we asked whether there were any particular rules in the house, in other words, things that their teenager must or must not do. The responses showed that many parents were concentrating on important issues. Most parents said that their teenager, for example, must say where they're going at night, and could not travel home alone late at night.

A rule of thumb is to establish rules that you can all live with, so that you don't waste your time and effort fighting long and tiring battles over minor issues.

One good example of this is tidy bedrooms. It can be extremely irritating for parents to see their teenager's bedroom in a complete mess. However, is it really worth the energy to cajole, insist, or even threaten them to keep their room tidy? It's probably better to keep your energy for major issues – things that you know really are important.

Parents have a right to make rules about behaviour which can threaten health or safety. Young people will usually appreciate that such rules are for their own benefit, and reflect their parents' care and concern for them. They will not feel like that about things which are petty. It is useful to remember, of course, that even the most important rules that you set do not have to be totally inflexible. If your rule is that your son or daughter must be home by a particular time at night, this deadline does not have apply to every night. If there is a party, for example, you may want to agree a later deadline for that occasion.

Having limits is all about negotiation and agreement. Some give and take on both sides is necessary to establish rules that really mean something. There is discussion of rules and structures, including what happens when agreements are broken, in Chapter 3.

The need to rebel

Rebellion is a word that many people associate with adolescence. However, it is worth stressing that most young people do not rebel against their parents in terms of all out war. What actually happens is something far less dramatic and more positive, involving young people moving towards independence and a different relationship with their parents. It does not, of course, always feel positive to parents!

The disagreements that occur in adolescence often give parents the feeling that everything they say and do is being challenged and rejected. This can be infuriating. It is, however, necessary in order for children to become adults. Teenagers need to develop their own identity and to separate themselves from their parents. Rebellion and making one's own decisions is all part of this. As one young person said to us:

> *... You don't want anything done for you anymore. You want to go as you please, how you please, do what you like.*

The ties that exist between parents and their children are very strong indeed. During adolescence, young people need to free themselves from the emotional ties of childhood. They have to break away in order to move on to be independent adults, and to have emotional relationships and ties outside the family. One way that many teenagers begin to break these ties is to persuade themselves that parents no longer have anything to offer. If parents are perceived as boring or wrong about everything, then there will not be much point in maintaining childhood ties with them. Imagine yourself in this situation: You have to change a relationship with someone close to you. It will be much easier if you can persuade yourself that the whole thing is a waste of time, and that you're better off out of it.

This is exactly what teenagers do. They try to make it easier for themselves by believing that they are better off without their parents' views and opinions. Clearly, it is not this simple. There is a lot of back and forth, a lot of uncertainty and inconsistency. Also, as we shall see later on, the rejection of parental views is often more superficial than real. It is worth remembering that teenage rebellion is most likely to be a psychological prop to make the tasks of separation somewhat easier to manage.

The need for time

Young children express their needs by crying, clinging, and asking for cuddles. Teenagers, on the other hand, express their needs by expecting (and demanding) time and attention from their parents – often at the most inconvenient moment. As one father told us:

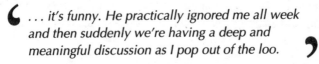

     ... it's funny. He practically ignored me all week and then suddenly we're having a deep and meaningful discussion as I pop out of the loo.

Many of the parents and teenagers we spoke to talked about the importance of parents giving young people time. One mother pointed out, however, that after a long working day it was hard to show any real interest in a teenager's problem or question. But it is worth making the effort. Teenagers are having to make difficult choices and decisions, they have worries and anxieties, and they are uncertain who they are. The advice of adults is essential. This is not to say that teenagers will always be prepared to listen to what their parents have to say. It often seems that young people are more interested in what their friends have to say, and it is sometimes a surprise for parents to be told that they are needed and that their time is valued.

Teenagers can be infuriating in this respect. They will often demand their parents' undivided attention on their own terms, often late at night or at the most inconvenient moment. If parents can manage it, however, the moments when young people really do want to talk can be the most rewarding of all. The time when a teenager seeks out their parent's opinion is often the time when they're most receptive to their parent's views and suggestions.

The need for privacy

Teenagers need privacy, because adolescence is a time of self-discovery. For this reason, young people may spend hours in front of the mirror or locked in the bedroom. This can be very irritating for mothers, fathers, and other household members. Teenagers may be examining themselves from all angles, writing diaries, or having secret thoughts and fantasies.

The problem with these activities for many parents is that they feel shut out, or worry that teenagers are hiding activities which are wrong or unacceptable. This is unlikely. They are more probably engaging in a normal and necessary process of self-discovery. Whether in the bathroom, in the bedroom, or outside, young people need to spend time on their own. Let them come to talk to you if and when they want to, but don't force them.

The need for room to grow

The task of parents is, in the end, to let go. This is not at all easy to do. Many parents invest in their children their own hopes,

expectations, and unfulfilled ambitions. There is no doubt, therefore, that much of the resistance of parents to letting their children
go is to do with the fear of loss – both of their children and of their
role as a parent. This is because for many parents, one of their
main roles in life is as a parent. The arrival of the teenage years
means that a child will soon be an independent adult. The loss of
the role of parent can be very difficult. There are, however, a
number of things that you can do as parents to make this process
easier:

- recognise that the way the family functions will have to
  change as your children become teenagers;
- give young people increasing opportunities, and let them
  take control over their own lives;
- make changes gradually, so that leaving home will not feel
  like too much of a loss, for parents or for teenagers.

In this way the changes of adolescence will feel more like a
gradual, and inevitable, move to a new relationship between you
and your teenager. As one young person said to us:

> It's quite difficult to draw the line. . . . In a way
> teenagers do want their parents to impose some sort
> of limits on them, but not unnecessarily. I mean, not
> to be treated as children, but not to be given so
> much responsibility that they don't know what to
> do with it.

We will talk more about issues of independence, rules and change
in the following chapter.

Further reading

A good book about the changes that happen to boys during puberty is Nick Fisher's *Boys about boys*, Pan, 1991.
A good book for girls which deals with the changes of puberty is Miriam Stoppard's *Everygirl's Lifeguide*, Dorling Kindersley, 1987.

Another good book for girls is by Lynda Madaras, *What's happening to my body?: A growing guide for parents and daughters*, Penguin, 1989.

Useful organisations

For confidential advice and information about all aspects of homosexuality, contact the **London Gay and Lesbian Switchboard.** It has information on local groups around the country. Parents of gay people are also welcome to phone. Tel. 0171-837-7324.

For information about sex education in schools, contact the **Sex Education Forum,** 8 Wakley Street, London, EC1V 7QE. Tel. 0171-843-6051/2.

CHAPTER THREE

Communication and family relationships

At the end of Chapter 1, we suggested that *communication* was essential to the development of good parent-teenager relationships. This chapter looks at the issue of communication and family relationships in more detail. It will include the following:

- Communication between parents and teenagers
- Decision-making in the family
- Giving increased responsibility
- Influences on young people
- Conflict in the family
- Rule-breaking and punishment

Communication between parents and teenagers

Communication between parents and teenagers is one of the areas of greatest difficulty during the teenage years. Yet it is fundamental to understanding and to improved relationships. This section looks at some of the barriers to good communication, and how they can be overcome.

Good communication between parents and teenagers is difficult for a number of reasons, including:

- the different values and attitudes of parents and teenagers;
- the fact that parents and teenagers will be communicating very different messages;
- young people's desire for greater freedom and independence;
- parents aiming to exercise some restraint over the rate at which their teenager is growing up;
- the images and stereotypes of the adolescent years.

As two of the parents we spoke to suggested:

> *When I tell people I've got teenage children they assume that therefore I have problems. They assume ... that there are bound to be big arguments and power struggles. It seems to me that that must actually make communication difficult.*

> *I think their need to be different is very important, and to be constantly criticised, which a lot of parents do with teenagers, with the way they dress, with the way they speak, or the friends they have ... is likely to discourage communication.*

Given that there are these barriers to good parent-teenager communication, what can be done to improve things?

We have compiled a list of dos and don'ts, based on suggestions from both the teenagers and the parents that we spoke to. These are listed below. Many of them are easier said than done of course, but they are useful clues to improving communication with teenagers. Do remember that communication involves much more than talking. An ability to listen, and a genuine respect for the young person's views, are key elements in ensuring that communication is a two-way street.

Don'ts

- **Don't try to score points.** Teenagers may seem brash and confident in their own ideas, but they are often quite the opposite. Like all of us, they don't like being put down; if they feel someone is going to be constantly scoring points off them, they may just clam up all together.
- **Don't push your ideas down their throats.** Attempts to impose ideas on young people are likely to be met with rejection.
- **Don't make snap judgements.** Many of the young people that we spoke to mentioned this. What they found particularly difficult was when parents make a judgement before they've even had a chance to give their point of view. This can of course be difficult to avoid when you're a parent; we often feel that a teenager simply doesn't have the experience to make a decision. But do try to listen to their point of view. They want to be seen as more adult, and their case needs to be listened to.

Dos

- **Do show some respect for the teenager's point of view.** Teenagers often complain that their point of view simply isn't acknowledged or given consideration. Sometimes we have to remind ourselves that adolescents are not children, and do often have good arguments to put forward. Acknowledging that their argument may sometimes be a good one is also necessary.
- **Do share your own experiences.** Most young people will appreciate a parent admitting that they have had to deal with a similar situation or experience. This is often a particularly good way to open up a conversation. This

doesn't mean detailing all your own experiences, but simply showing that you are aware of the difficulties of many aspects of the teenage years. Sometimes teenagers will forget that you were their age once too; it can be useful to remind them.

- **Do make time to listen.** As we have already said, giving young people time is very important. It is in fact essential for good communication to take place. If teenagers feel that parents are rushing about, with lots of things to do, they may feel that they are simply not able to talk. We mustn't forget that however brash teenagers may seem, most want and need to talk to their parents. A feeling that parents will give them time is essential.

- **Do respect the young person's need for privacy.** There will be many times when your teenager will not want to talk. As we said in the last chapter, time to be alone is an essential part of adolescence. Try not to feel rejected or shut out. Be ready for when your teenager does want to talk, but don't try to make them do so.

- **Do try to act as a role model for your teenager.** Provide them with some examples of good communication. During disagreements with your partner or friends, teenagers will want to see how you deal with the situation. Show that you can listen, and are willing to negotiate; try not to lose your temper or resort to name calling.

- **Do remember that communication doesn't always need words.** Communication between parents and teenagers can take the form of a hug or an arm around the shoulder, or taking the time out to do an activity together.

Some comments from teenagers on this topic demonstrate these points well:

 ... the main thing is to be impartial and not form moral judgements about things. Cos as soon as you

*make a moral judgement about something then it's
impossible to talk about it or resolve the problem
really . . .*

*They've got to have the patience to sit down and
try and understand.*

*The teenager's got to try and understand why the
parents hassle them or why they don't want to do
something. Most parents mean it well-heartedly
but they don't know how to put it across.*

*. . . even though at times they may not feel like
talking about a problem a teenager has, if she brings
herself round to talking to them, even if they don't
feel like talking it's important that they show the
child that they are interested in them . . .*

Developing good communication between you and your
teenager is one part of effective decision-making. It is this that we
turn to now.

Decision-making in the family

The points above should lead to more relaxed and rewarding discussions between parents and teenagers. Good communication is
particularly important when it comes to decision-making. All families, of whatever kind, have to make decisions. These might be
about major things such as whether to move house or where to go
on holiday, or they may be about smaller things such as what to
watch on TV, or whether to buy a new piece of furniture.

In families with young children, most decisions will be taken by
parents. As children become adolescents however, they will
expect to play an increasing role in family decision-making.

Furthermore they will demand more freedom to make decisions about their own lives. It's often difficult to get the balance right in terms of decision-making. How much freedom should young people have to make their own decisions? How does decision-making change with increasing age? What happens when parents feel a young person does not have the knowledge or experience to decide about things for themselves?

Adults should not simply lay down the law. As one parent said to us:

> ❝ ... if you want something to go your way the best way to do it I've felt is to suggest, but not make the decision, not to say "we're going to do so and so" but to put it "what do you think about doing so and so? I think it would be a good idea because of so and so" and let it ride. But if you say "we are going to do so and so" they will say no. ❞

As we have said already, there is nothing more likely to create conflict than for adults to impose their own rules and regulations irrespective of the needs of the young person concerned. This may in fact encourage teenagers to break the rules at the first opportunity.

On the other hand, parents should not give up and leave the teenager to make the decisions. It is of course tempting to do this, especially when you are involved in a long and tiring battle with your son or daughter. All the research evidence available shows that this is the last thing that teenagers need or want. It suggests to them that a parent no longer cares what happens.

Discussion and negotiation with teenagers

Without doubt the best way for parents to proceed in decision-making is through discussion, negotiation, and compromise. One parent described to us how she used negotiation:

❦ *What time to go to bed and what time to come home at night ... I actually discovered quite by accident that if I said "what time do you think?" they generally suggested a time that was earlier than I had thought of suggesting. So I considered this to be a superb way of negotiating.* ❞

The teenagers that we spoke to often said that this was exactly what they wanted – to be able to talk about something and come to an agreed decision about it. What the young people we spoke to particularly resented was being lectured to, and being told the outcome before the discussion had even begun. As one young person said to us:

❦ *I hate mum just saying "This is the decision" like she did when I was five. She wants me to grow up, and most of the time she helps, but I hate it when she just tells me the decision.* ❞

As in any other relationship, it is also important for parents to be consistent. As this father very clearly put it:

❦ *[Young people] need you to be consistent. Not "yes you can do this" one day, and then "no you can't do it" the next. It's important that, isn't it? So they know that you mean things, that there are rules.* ❞

We said in Chapter 2 that an important aspect of decision-making, and of establishing rules and guidelines, is for parents to focus their efforts on the really important issues. Health and safety is a good example. Try to concentrate on these issues, and not to dwell on others – such as tidy bedrooms or household chores – which may seem important, but probably aren't really.

Try also to justify your stand to a teenager. Although they may resent these rules at the time, the underlying message is likely to get through – that the parent cares, and is concerned about their son or daughter's well-being. This is likely to be of positive benefit in the long run.

You must be prepared to negotiate with your teenager. They need to see that you are open and flexible, that you will listen to their viewpoint, and that you will justify your arguments. If parents are unyielding and stubborn, their offspring are likely to approach rules and negotiations in much the same way. If parents are flexible, then young people are more likely to be so too. This is a good model for them to copy when dealing with other people in the future.

Giving increased responsibility

Decision-making and negotiating with teenagers is likely to be easier if parents increase a young person's independence and responsibility over time. Decision-making with a twelve-year-old is very different to decision-making with a seventeen-year-old. Making changes to a family's rules and regulations can be difficult. Growing is a gradual process, and if parents are able to make adjustments to keep pace with their teenager's needs, then it will probably be much easier to handle any problems and conflicts that occur.

One mother that we spoke to described how this worked with her daughter. She and her husband had always been quite adamant that her daughter should not drink alcohol while she was young. By the time she'd reached sixteen and had started going out with friends, however, they felt that this rule had to be changed:

> ❛ ... at sixteen we couldn't tell her "you can't drink",
> because we know she will. So we say, well,
> have one or two drinks only, and she does.
> There's no point saying "now here's the rules, take
> them or leave them". Because she'll probably
> leave them ... ❜

This is an important point. At a younger age, a parent may simply tell their son or daughter what they can or can't do, where they can and can't go. Trying to do this with older teenagers simply will not work.

Teenagers need to prove that they're growing up, prove that they can take on new responsibilities. As teenagers get older, they need more responsibility – whether it's to manage their own time or finances, or to decide what they eat, drink, or do in their leisure time. Parents have to accept this, and amend rules and regulations to adapt to it.

Influences on young people

Parents want to be able to influence their sons or daughters. They want to help them make wise decisions about their futures, to keep safe and healthy, and to develop good and satisfying relationships. Often in adolescence, however, influencing young people seems a very difficult thing to do.

We have already talked about a number of ways in which you can encourage your teenager to take notice of what you say. The list of dos and don'ts we gave on pages 28–29 is likely to be a good start to this. There are other means, however, by which parents can exert influence. Some of these are given below.

Flexibility and openness

The point about flexibility is worth re-stating here. Being too dogmatic about your views is most likely to lead to young people rejecting them outright. They are far more likely to take some note of your opinions if they feel they have some freedom of choice about whether to accept them or not. One teenager told us that the best way for parents to get their message across was:

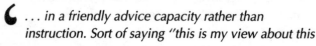 *... in a friendly advice capacity rather than instruction. Sort of saying "this is my view about this*

> *. . . but if you don't agree with it then it's fair enough".* **"**

Overstating the point rarely works with teenagers, as it is likely to provoke rebellion and a resistance to parental views altogether. Although this can be difficult at times, do try to remember that your views will be taken much more seriously if they are

- understated;
- presented as a number of options;
- as free as possible from a 'parents knows best' position.

The importance of listening

Listening also has a strong impact on the degree of influence that parents have on their teenagers. If a parent is able to listen, and to take seriously the opinions of a teenager, then it is likely that in turn the teenager will feel more able to listen and to take seriously other people's opinions. This has a lot to do with the fact that if someone shows you that they respect and value your viewpoint, then you are more likely to think highly of them as well.

Communication is one of the skills that young people learn in the teenage years. How people relate to each other within the family – whether it's mothers, fathers, siblings, or grandparents – will be noticed by teenagers. If adults in the family are willing to listen to teenagers, to give them time and attention, then the message that they are valued will come through clearly. Developing mutual respect is important. It is essential when it comes to discussing important topics like drug or alcohol use, or sexual activity. Influence over teenagers cannot be demanded or imposed; rather it must be worked at and developed.

> **"** *. . . if it's something like drugs or something like that, I'll listen to my mum . . . because she can give me a better view. If it's clothes then my friends – or politics – I listen to them as well as my parents.* **"**

Types of influence

It is important to add here that there are different types of influence. We have been talking so far about fairly direct influence, where parents talk with their teenagers about the things that affect them.

There are other forms of influence that parents can have. These include acting as a role model for teenagers. If, as we have said, parents show that they can listen, negotiate, and act considerately, teenagers are more likely to do the same. Influence can also be exerted on young people more indirectly, by involving an older sibling or relative whom the young person might listen to.

The influence of friends

It is important to discuss the role of friends and the peer group when talking about the influences on young people's views and behaviours. Friends – and the wider peer group – will exert pressures on young people to behave in certain ways. Some young people will be more easily influenced than others.

This is not a simple issue. Young people are not influenced only by parents or only by friends. They are influenced by both. The issue of the influence of friends on teenagers is an important one, and we will look at it in detail in the next chapter.

Conflict in the family

Conflict is an inevitable part of human life. Families are not immune from this, and a certain amount of disagreement and conflict is inevitable.

Conflict in families can take many forms. It may be between a parent and teenager. It may also be between siblings, step-children and step-parents, or between partners. Such conflict can be draining and upsetting, but it is important to try to deal with conflict when it happens, so that it is not allowed to permanently affect relationships within the family.

Family members may disagree over life-styles and values, or freedom and restrictions. They may also disagree about something which is in short supply – money or somebody's time for example – or the family may be changing and members may find it difficult to adapt to new relationships.

Conflict will also have different forms, and different causes, depending on the age of the teenager. A thirteen-year-old may disagree with parents about doing their homework, or the amount of pocket money they receive. A seventeen-year-old may disagree about whether they can stay out late at a party, or whether a new boyfriend or girlfriend can stay overnight. The age of the teenager will affect how you deal with the conflict, and will influence the nature of the punishment when rules are broken. Although it is hard to appreciate at the time, some conflicts can also be positive, clarifying people's positions and letting family members know how others feel.

There are a number of ways in which conflict can be tackled. Often it is tempting to try the 'easy' option. This might be to lay down the law and refuse to discuss an issue, or it may be to just give in to your son or daughter. These strategies rarely work in practice. And even if they work once, imposing your view or giving in all the time will not be good for family relationships in the long-term.

Conflict has to be managed by parents. It can be very time-consuming, and exhausting, and it can involve hurt feelings and anger.

The following steps may help to settle a conflict:

- **Agree to tackle the problem.** Arrange a place and a time when you and your daughter/son can talk undisturbed. Agree between you that you will try to sort the problem out.
- **Set some ground rules.** Agree that you will listen to each other, without shouting or name calling.

- **Explain how you both feel.** Let each party explain their point of view and how they feel. Try not to interrupt each other. Talk through the issues, and make sure you understand the other person's position.
- **Look at the options.** Talk through what the options could be to solve the problem. For example if the problem is about a parent feeling their daughter is going out too much, some of the options could be for her to (1) go out only at weekends or on weekdays (2) to go out only after she's completed homework and/or household tasks (3) to spend two nights a week at home.
- **Agree on one – or more – of the options.** You and your son/daughter can then select the option(s) you feel might work. You may pick the same, or different, ones. You will probably have to negotiate to get agreement. In the above example, it may be for the adolescent to go out no more than three evenings on weekdays.
- **Write out the agreement.** This helps to formalise the arrangement, and allows you to decide later whether either side has broken the agreement. You should also talk about what the penalties will be if your daughter breaks the agreement.

These strategies should help you and your teenager to reach agreements that you can both accept.

Despite trying to settle a conflict in this way, you may not be able to get any agreement with your teenager. They may, for example, continue to stay out late and not tell you where they are, or repeatedly not do the homework that they've been set. There are a number of things that you can try in this situation:

- Take another look at the issue. How important is it really? Do you really want or need to pursue it?
- If you feel you can, then back off. You may hate to do it, but if it's not really that important, then let the issue drop.
- If you think the issue is really important, then put your foot

down, and decide on a punishment. Some of the options for punishment are discussed next.

Rule-breaking and punishment

There will still of course be times when your agreed rules are broken. What should you do then? The following points are important ground-rules for punishment:

- Be fair – did your son or daughter know what the rules were in the first place, and so understand why you're punishing them?
- Be firm – don't let rule-breaking go unpunished. Show your son or daughter that agreements need to be kept, and that you will act when they break them.
- Be reasonable – make the punishment fit the crime. Try not to be harsh in your punishment.

There are a number of different ways of punishing teenagers. Some of the methods used by the parents that we spoke to included the following:

- Grounding – this involves not allowing your son or daughter to go out for a certain number of evenings or weekends. The more serious the problem the longer they are grounded for. This can be a very effective strategy. As one mother told us:

... it links their action to a consequence. We agreed he'd be home by 9.30, and he strolls in at 11.00 saying he felt like staying on for a while. So I grounded him for the next five days. It's made him realise he can't just pick and choose betwen the agreements he wants to stick to and those he doesn't.

- Withdrawal of a treat – a number of parents said that they
  withdrew something when their son or daughter broke an
  agreed rule. This could involve not allowing them to go out
  to a disco or party, or on a school or family trip.
- Being given extra tasks to do – a young person may be
  punished by being given extra household tasks, such as
  cleaning or washing up, for a fixed period of time.
- Reduced or no pocket-money for a fixed period of time.

The strategies above can be effective in helping your daughter
or son to learn that rules are there for a reason, and that there are
consequences involved in breaking rules. This is a lesson which
will prove useful for them later in life too.

Two things, finally, are important in thinking about rule-breaking and punishment with teenagers. First, in conflict situations you
will often have your own anger to deal with as well as having to
deal with your son or daughter. A twelve-year-old may carelessly
damage a valued object; a seventeen-year-old may stay out late
without telling you. Both these events will make you angry, and
understandably so. You may then react suddenly and irrationally
as a result. One way of dealing with this is to give yourself some
space. For example tell your teenager that you want to talk about
the issue in the morning. It'll give you time to cool down and think
more rationally about what you should do. Dealing with the event
at the time may make you say and do things that you regret later.
Of course there will be times when your anger takes over – this is
natural. But giving yourself some space and time to think may help
you make decisions that you're happier with in the long run.

Secondly, it is important to remember that dealing with rule-
breaking and punishment is never straightforward. Some young people will consistently flout rules and agreements, apparently immune
to any punishment you give. This is very draining for parents. Here
are a couple of strategies that parents can try in these circumstances:

- Involve another adult, perhaps one of your friends or a
  teacher, to see if they can get through to the teenager.

- Contact a professional organisation like Parentline or Exploring Parenthood. Their addresses and telephone numbers are listed at the end of Chapter 1.

If you are going through a difficult time with your teenager, remember that things will change. What may seen like an impossible situation will next week appear to be more manageable. Some of the things we have covered in this chapter may be helpful. Keep things in perspective, and if your son or daughter is making you angry or upset, do try to stand back from the turmoil. You can help best by not letting yourself get wound up by behaviour that probably has little to do with you, but a lot to do with the frustrations of adolescence.

Further reading

A good book which looks at how to improve communication between parents and teenagers is by E Fenwick and T Smith: *Adolescence: The survival guide for parents*, Dorling Kindersley, 1993. It includes case studies of families with teenagers.

CHAPTER FOUR

Friends and peers

This chapter looks at the issues surrounding teenagers' friends and friendship. It includes the following:

- Teenagers' friends and friendship
- Friends and parents
- Peer influence and pressure
- Bullying

Teenagers' friends and friendship

Friends are important to everybody, but especially to young people. If we think back to our own childhood and adolescence, this should remind us just how important friends are.

In childhood friends are generally people who play together. Young children have little sense of friends having needs or feelings different to their own. By adolescence this has changed. Teenagers have a much more realistic sense of other people as being different from themselves, with different views, ideas and needs. During adolescence young people also learn that relationships are reciprocal – they can get things from friends, but they have to give something as well.

Friends play a very important part in a teenager's development. Teenagers usually become involved with a *group* of friends. These groups normally see themselves, or try to make themselves, different from other groups in some way – by their appearance, what they talk about, what they do. Being part of friendship groups helps young people to begin to move away from parents and towards independence.

Being a member of a friendship group provides many positive experiences for a teenager, including:

- being with other people who are going through the same uncertainties and experiences as they are;
- learning how to relate to other people and develop relationships;
- providing a source of support, advice, and information.

The nature of friendship also changes throughout the teenage years. In early adolescence most young people will go around with a group of the same sex, often boys or girls from the area they live in, or from school. Later in adolescence – usually around age fourteen or fifteen – male and female groups will start to mix more, and some young people will start going out and having relationships. By late adolescence most young people will have a variety of friends, both male and female.

Friends and parents

Teenagers' friends can make parents uneasy or anxious, and parents may feel jealous or neglected as their son or daughter spends increasing amounts of time with friends. Many parents feel anxious that friends are a bad influence on their son or daughter.

However, there are a number of ways that parents can keep a caring eye on their offspring and their friends, without appearing to interfere:

- **Don't assume the worst.** Difficult as it is, don't assume that your son's or daughter's friends are invevitably going to be difficult or a bad influence, just because of their appearance or how they spend their time. Try not to comment negatively on your teenager's friends, especially about how they look. If you do your teenager may well try to distance you from them.
- **Make friends welcome in the home.** Parents can be more vigilant about their child's friends if they meet them regularly. Make sure your daughter or son feels able to invite their friends round. Show an interest in their friends, talk to them, find out more about them. This will not only allow you to keep an eye on who your teenager is spending time with, but also suggest that parents and friends are not living in two completely separate worlds.
- **Give them some freedom.** Teenagers and their friends spend a lot of time talking, gossiping, and sharing experiences. Spending a whole evening sitting in their bedroom may seem a waste of time to parents, but it's very important to teenagers. Try not to persuade them to 'do something' if they are happy just being with each other.

You may still feel concerned that your daughter or son is getting in with the wrong crowd. If so, there are a number of things that you can do:

- **Talk to them about it, calmly and carefully.** Don't criticise or ridicule their friends. Try to understand what they enjoy about being with their friends, and explain your uncertainties or concerns.
- **Ask them about what they do with their friends.** Do they ever do anything dangerous or illegal? Do they ever feel

pressurised to do things that they don't want to do? Do they need to talk about how they can say 'no'?

- **Stress that you're asking because you're concerned about them.** Make sure your teenager knows that if he or she does have problems or worries about friends, they can tell you about it. Your teenager needs to know that you're there if things start to go wrong.

There are other times when you may, justifiably, feel concerned about your son's or daughter's friends and relationships. These include

- an adolescent who seems to have no friends;
- an adolescent who suddenly withdraws from or loses interest in his or her friends;
- an adolescent who is secretive about friends and his or her activities with them.

In all these cases, there may be a straightforward explanation. The teenager may have had an argument and fallen out with a group of friends, or they may feel that a parent won't like some new friends and so be reluctant to bring them home. There may be other reasons for these behaviours however, such as bullying or involvement in drug use. You may want to speak to your teenager's school about your fears, or seek advice from a professional organisation.

Peer influence and pressure

We have already said that friends and the peer group play an important role in adolescent development. This is worth restating. The general view is that friends have a negative influence on young people. However, friends can often be a positive influence on teenagers, for example by encouraging them *not* to become involved in anti-social or delinquent activity.

❝ *If you want to be an individual and you don't want
to mix in with the peer group then that's very
stressful.* ❞

It is important not to see the parents/friends debate as an
either/or one. As we showed in Chapter 1, research has shown that
most young people have quite similar views to their parents on
major issues like politics or work values. It's in areas like clothes
and music that teenagers are more likely to follow their friends.

Teenagers are more likely to turn to their peers when they feel
their parents:

- are not interested in them;
- don't have information about something that interests or
  concerns them;
- are not willing to talk to them about something, such as
  drugs or sex.

Or, teenagers may turn to peers if they:

- feel they have no support at home;
- lack self-confidence;
- don't have one or two close friends who provide support.

A teenager's susceptibility to peer pressure is also dependent on
other factors, including:

- how much they need to fit in with the group;
- their confidence and ability to resist peer pressure;
- their age.

Research has shown that young people are most open to peer
pressure in middle adolescence, around the age of thirteen or fourteen. After that age, peer influence is reduced.

Parents can play a key role in helping their teenager to resist
peer pressure to get involved in dangerous or illegal activities.
There are a number of things parents can do:

- **Talk with them about situations involving friends which might arise in the future and which they might find difficult.** Adolescents often feel unprepared for the pressure their friends put on them. Talk about what they might do in different hypothetical situations, like if their friends start getting involved in vandalism or stealing from shops.
- **Discuss situations where you have had to deal with pressure from friends or peers.** Talk about your own adolescence, or pressures in your work or social life. Most people have had to deal with peer pressure at some point. This will encourage your son or daughter to think about situations that might arise, and about how they can deal with them.
- **Promote responsibility and decision-making.** Let your son or daughter begin to make their own decisions, and listen to their point of view. This will encourage them to act more independently and responsibly amongst their peers. Young people who have always been told what to do at home will not expect to have to make their own decisions out of the home.
- **Let them know that you are there if they do get into problems with their friends.** Teenagers need to know that you are there for them, and that they can talk to you. Going against the peer group is never easy, and young people need to have support to do it.

Other things that you might do if you are concerned about the influence of friends on your teenager include talking to other parents, approaching your teenager's school, or contacting a support group for parents.

Bullying

Bullying takes place in many different contexts – in schools, youth clubs, work, even in the family. It can also take many forms. It

TEENAGERS IN THE FAMILY

may involve threatening someone to get their money or possessions, verbal abuse (name-calling and offensive remarks), or it can
involve physical attacks. It can be done by one individual against
another, or by a group of people. Bullying can make its victims
feel isolated, afraid, and even suicidal.

There are a number of signs that could indicate that a teenager
is being bullied. Be aware if your child:

- becomes particularly anxious or depressed;
- doesn't want to go to school, to a youth club, or to work;
- wants to change a regular route suddenly, or change the
  mode of transport;
- has a sudden increase in cuts or bruises;
- frequently says he or she has lost money or prized
  possessions.

It is very important to take bullying seriously, and not to dismiss
it or assume that your son or daughter can handle it. If you suspect
bullying, the first thing to do is to talk to your son or daughter. Let
them know that you are interested and concerned. The teenager
may be reluctant to talk or may be frightened, especially if they've
been threatened. Encourage them to talk to you. You need to
know what the problem is, how they feel, and what help you can
give. They may well have been bottling it up, and so will need
time to tell you about it, and perhaps get upset or cry. Remind
them that they do not have to cope alone, and that you will help
them through it.

There are a number of things that you can do to help your
teenager if they are being bullied. However, telling your teenager's
school or youth club, and demanding that they do something
about it, does not always help. It may also not be what your son or
daughter wants you to do.

Start by discussing what is actually happening with your son or
daughter. There are a number of strategies that you can encourage
them to try:

- Can they avoid being in the same place as the bully?
- Can they use certain verbal replies or physical stances to show the bully that they're not being upset or frightened by the bullying?
- Can they get other friends to help them by showing solidarity?

Your teenager will need your help in trying out these strategies. Talk to them about what happens, and make sure that they know that you will help them work it out if these strategies don't stop the bullying.

Schools and bullying

For many adolescents, bullying happens at school. Most schools in Britain now have a whole-school policy on bullying, or particular strategies to combat it. Some schools have bullying councils or committees, where staff and pupils get together to try to deal with bullies. When bullying happens at school, most schools usually recommend that:

- teenagers are encouraged to talk to a teacher or senior member of staff, with a parent present if they wish;
- parents arrange to speak with the headteacher or senior staff separately if they wish;
- parents don't confront the bullies or their parents personally.

It may help first to find out whether your son or daughter has a particular teacher whom they feel they can trust, and whom they can talk to about the bullying. Offer to go with them to see this teacher if that would help.

You can also help by getting some books or other information for your son or daughter to read. This will give them the strength to tackle the problem, and also serve to remind them that other people are concerned about the problem. There are also a number of professional organisations who can help young people who are being bullied. These resources and organisations are listed at the end of the chapter.

If your teenager is a bully

All bullying is done by someone. You may discover that your son or daughter is a bully. Difficult as this can be to accept, it has to be dealt with. A child who bullies other children does so for a reason, and neglecting those reasons may well lead to more serious problems for the bully later on.

A number of strategies can be used to stop your adolescent bullying others:

- Try to talk to them about it. What is it they are doing? What do they get from it, and how does it make them feel? Why do they do it?
- Encourage them to think about how it makes the victim feel. Get them to recall times when they felt lonely or afraid.
- Show that you disapprove. Your adolescent may appear to be resistant, but they will be influenced by your viewpoint.

Bullying can be particularly damaging for teenagers. No young person should have to endure bullying, and no young person should be allowed to bully another. Parents, teenagers and teachers need to work together to deal with bullying.

In concluding this chapter, it is worth stressing the importance of friends and friendship to young people. With all the changes that occur in the adolescent years, teenagers need the company, support and friendship of others who are going through the same uncertainties and experiences. Friends can be a negative influence on young people – and we have suggested ways that you can help your son or daughter to resist and deal with negative influences – but friends can also play a very positive role in young people's development into adulthood.

Further reading

A useful book about schools and bullying is by Michele Elliot: *Bullying – A practical guide to coping in schools*, Longman, 1991.

A pack on bullying, which is aimed at families, is called *Bullying and how to fight it*. It's available from SCRE, 15 St John Street, Edinburgh, EH8 8JR. Tel. 0131-557-2944.

Useful organisations

The **Anti-Bullying Campaign (ABC)** provides information and advice on bullying, as well as publications. Contact it at 10 Borough High Street, London, SE1 9QQ. Tel. 0171-378-1446 (between 9.30 and 5 weekdays).

CHAPTER FIVE

Teenagers in changing families

This chapter looks at the family, and changes that occur within families. It includes the following:

- The changing family
- Separation and divorce
- Single parenthood
- Stepfamilies
- Death in the family

The changing family

Family life in Britain today is very different from the way it was twenty years ago. The number of people who live in a traditional nuclear family has dramatically declined in this period. In the early 1970s, 92 per cent of families with dependent children were headed by a married or cohabiting couple. By 1991 this figure had dropped to 81 per cent. One in five children are now living in lone-parent families.

This is largely a result of the sharp increase in family breakdown and divorce. The divorce rate in Britain has doubled since 1971. One in three marriages now ends in divorce, and half of second marriages also fail. Each year, 150,000 children and young people will see their parents separate or divorce. Many of these families become part of step-families – six million people in Britain now live in a stepfamily.

Many young people will therefore experience a change in their family circumstances during their teenage years, as a result of a natural parent leaving the family home, or of becoming part of a step-family. Some will become part of a lone-parent family; others will find themselves shuttling between two family homes.

Families may also become involved in adoption and fostering. These families have to deal with many of the issues that step-families face, learning to adapt to and live with a new person in the home. They also have to deal with the difficulties, anxieties, and possibly the behavioural problems of a child or young person with an unsettled life so far. There are a number of organisations which can provide help and support to those involved in fostering and adoption – see the organisations listed at the end of this chapter.

As well as separation, divorce, and re-marriage, other events may affect a teenager's family life. The death of someone in the family – a parent, sibling, or most often a grand-parent – will change the way teenagers see their family, and the relationships that they have within it. Dealing with death and bereavement is difficult at any age – during adolescence it can be particularly hard.

Separation and divorce

Parental separation and/or divorce is not easy for anyone involved, but it can be particularly difficult for teenagers.

However, all the evidence shows that most teenagers eventually re-adjust after family breakdown, especially if parents follow a number of guidelines (which are discussed below). Research also shows that teenagers are much better able to get through a divorce than to live with chronic family conflict. This section looks at how parents can help teenagers through a divorce or family breakdown.

Helping teenagers through divorce

When parents have decided that they are definitely going to get separated or divorced, there are a number of things that they can do to help their teenagers through it. Most of these hinge on giving young people information, so that they know what's going on. One teenager that we interviewed had had a particularly bad experience:

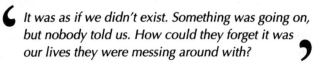

It was as if we didn't exist. Something was going on, but nobody told us. How could they forget it was our lives they were messing around with?

The following guidelines are important to help young people through divorce:

- Let the teenager know what's going to happen as soon as you have decided. Don't let them hear about it during a row between you, or from friends or relations.
- If possible, explain carefully to your teenager why you have decided to separate. Agree with your partner, if you can, what you're going to say to your children in advance. Try not to allocate blame to each other or start an argument.
- Involve young people in decisions about their future. Teenagers will obviously be anxious about where they will live and who they will live with. They will also want to know how often they will see the parent that they don't live with.
- Keep the teenager properly informed about events as they progress – for example about decisions to sell the house, or

55

for one parent to move out. Answer their questions, however trivial they may seem to you. Worries about money, or pets, are important to teenagers, especially younger ones.

Reactions to divorce

Teenagers will, of course, react in different ways to their parents' decision to separate and/or divorce. For some the news may come as a relief, a sign of the end of years of arguing or violence between their parents. For most though, the news will probably make them feel upset, anxious, and confused.

Teenagers will express their feelings about the separation in different ways. These may include:

- sadness and withdrawal, perhaps spending a lot of time alone in their bedroom;
- throwing themselves into social or sporting events;
- reverting to child-like behaviour;
- anger or aggression towards one or both parents.

These emotions will last for different lengths of time. A feeling of security – that they know what is happening, and that their parents care about them – will help young people to come through the separation.

Research has shown that one to two years after a separation or divorce, most teenagers are no more disturbed or troubled than those from intact families. There is some evidence, however, that boys have more difficulty adjusting to family breakdown than girls. Boys may therefore need particular help and support during this time.

Life after divorce

The period after the separation or divorce is central to a teenager's adjustment. Parents can do a number of things to help their teenager. These can be usefully summarised as some dos and don'ts.

TEENAGERS IN THE FAMILY

We'll start with the don'ts:

- **Don't** always criticize your ex-partner. Teenagers need to feel positively about both their mother and father. Hearing your mother or father constantly described as useless or stupid is unfair on teenagers.
- **Don't** use your teenager as a messenger between you and your ex-partner. If you have something to say to him or her – for example about being short of money, or that you don't like their new partner – phone or write to them.
- **Don't** ever blame your teenager for the separation. Having a parent say 'that's the sort of behaviour that made your father leave' will be painful for teenagers, and may make them feel responsible for the ending of their parents' relationship. Teenagers often feel their parents' separation has something to do with their behaviour anyway. These sorts of comments just make these feelings worse.
- **Don't** use your teenager to score points. If your ex-partner has said that your son or daughter can't have a particular treat because they've broken an agreed rule, then support them in that. Don't let your son or daughter do something or have something just to spite your ex-partner.

I think it was the hate between the two of them. Knowing how much they hated each other and being in the middle of that. That was really awful ... They were really so horrible to each other all the time, and all they'd do was slag each other off to me. And I hated it, I really hated it. I felt really in the middle and like I couldn't do anything. I think at first I felt like part of it was my fault and I should have stopped it, but, I mean, I just couldn't. But I always carry it around, that I should have been able to stop it.

Now here are some dos:

- **Do** remind your teenager that although as, parents, you may no longer love each other, you both still love them.
- **Do** talk to your ex-partner about your son or daughter, and make joint decisions about your teenager's life. For example, if you agree that the teenager cannot stay out after 10pm on weekdays, make sure that both parents enforce this when the teenager is with them.
- **Do** make sure the teenager realises that there is not going to be a reconciliation between you. Maintaining a forlorn hope and having it dashed can be very distressing for teenagers.
- **Do** talk to your teenager about the possibility of either one of you forming a new relationship, or getting remarried at some point. Knowing that this is a possibility will probably make it easier for the teenager if it does happen.
- **Do** prepare yourself for the fact that if the children live with you, your ex-partner may lose contact with the children over time, or disappear suddenly. Remember that many teenagers will blame themselves for this, and they will need considerable support to come to terms with the loss.

Single parenthood

One in five families in Britain is a lone parent family. Although a small proportion are headed by men, the majority are headed by women. Most of these women are separated, divorced or widowed.

Being a single parent isn't easy. Single parents have to do all the things that two or more people would otherwise do. Lone parents manage household finances, sort out living arrangements, manage childcare, and many have full- or part-time jobs.

Having a teenager in the family can be difficult for single parents. If the single parent doesn't have a partner, they have to make decisions and deal with any crises themselves, and be the one who provides practical help and a listening ear for their teenager. This can be very draining, especially on top of all the other tasks that single parents have to manage.

However, a teenager in the family need be no more difficult for a single parent than for two parents. It depends on the parent's relationship with their son or daughter, and the resources and support available to them. In the interviews, many separated and single parents said it was simply important to hang on in there, and to remember that things will get better.

One of the most difficult areas for single parents can be setting boundaries for their teenagers and monitoring them. Yet teenagers need rules and guidelines, especially following the uncertainty of a separation. One mother explained to us how she coped:

In the first few months I was far too soft and fuzzy about my boundaries. I was really going through a hard emotional time, and they were pushing me and testing me out and seeing how far they could go. You sort of feel guilty. I think it's when you don't know where you are and you feel guilty because you've separated. Once I'd firmed up, and I knew where I stood, then the children knew where I stood and then they weren't out of control at all.

One of the main issues for single parents is discipline and control. It is often difficult for single parents to monitor their teenager. Encouraging responsibility and safe behaviour amongst teenagers is therefore essential. One single mother we spoke to described her relationship with her son:

... he sees his father regularly, but they're not close. So really I'm the only one who can give him advice and support. He had a phase when he was out all

*the time, and a bit wild. It was hard, but we
talked a lot. I let him know I was worried.* **,**

There are a number of organisations who offer help and advice
to single parents. These are listed at the end of this chapter.

Step-families

Step-families take many forms. A step-family may include for
example:

- a mother or father who is separated or widowed, and her or
  his children, and a new partner who moves into the family
  home;
- two parents who each have children from a previous
  relationship, and who decide to live together or get married;
- two parents each with children from a previous relationship,
  who subsequently have their own children.

Step-families are therefore best described as families who have
additional parents and possibly additional children too. A step-
father or step-mother may move into the role of a teenager's real
parent, who may have left the family home or have died. The natural parent may or may not be in contact with his or her children.

Step-families are, at least initially, characterised by uncertain
relationships and divided loyalties. Teenagers and step-parents are
unsure about their role, about how they should behave, and about
how they feel. Many step-families experience a two-stage process
of initial reactions (and often quite acute difficulties), followed by
the development of more settled relationships.

Initial reactions

Early on, having a step-parent in the family can be very difficult for
all involved. Teenagers' initial reactions will often be hostile. This
may be because of embarrassment – not knowing how to relate to

the new person – or resentment – feeling that a natural parent is being replaced.

In the early stages, teenagers' uncertainty and resentment will probably encourage them to test out the new parent. Teenagers will be wondering whether the house 'rules' have been changed, and whether they'll be able to get round the new parent to their advantage. The teenager may be awkward, questioning and hostile towards the step-parent. This is obviously difficult for step-parents, as well as for the remaining natural parent, but it is worth trying to remember that this phase will probably be short-lived.

> You have to work a bit harder with step-children. You can't just say "do this because I say so" as they'll probably tell you that you're not their mother and they don't have to do what you say ... I've always tried to explain decisions to them, and discuss things with them, and that's normally worked.

The teenager's natural parent has a very important role to play in helping to develop a good relationship between their new partner and their son or daughter. The teenager needs to know that they are still loved and valued by the natural parent. This can be done by

- spending time alone with them;
- doing activities together that they did before the separation from or death of the other natural parent;
- supporting the teenager – if appropriate – when there is a dispute with the step-parent.

Developing relationships

It normally takes a long time for good relationships to develop between people. Between teenagers and step-parents, it can take longer.

In order for acceptance and affection to develop between step-parents and teenagers, step-parents can do a number of things. Again, there are a number of dos and don'ts.

First the don'ts:

- **Don't** expect a good relationship to develop overnight. It will probably take months or even years, with some unpleasantness on the way. Be patient.
- **Don't** compete with the teenager's natural parent. Try not to criticize the natural parent, or feel offended or awkward when they are being discussed.
- **Don't** feel guilty if you don't hit it off immediately with your step-children, or you don't feel very warm towards them. They are individuals too, and you need to know their good and bad points.
- **Don't** try to bribe the teenager, for example by regularly buying them gifts or letting them do whatever they want.

Now here are some dos:

- **Do** spend time with the step-children, doing things that will bring you together – for example playing sports, or going to see films.
- **Do** try to sort out arguments between yourself and your step-children without asking their natural parent to intervene. You need to develop some authority of your own.
- **Do** respect a teenager's privacy. You need to give them space and time to get used to having you about. Wanting to be in their room when you are in the lounge may not actually be anything personal.
- **Do** show them that you care for them, and that you want to be part of their lives.
- **Do** be yourself. Don't try to be someone that you think they will like.

Building a good relationship with a new partner, and with other people's children, can be difficult. It is certainly a long-term process. Many step-families, however, are characterised by warm and loving relationships.

Death in the family

The death of someone close to you is painful at any age. For young people it can be particularly difficult, because of teenagers' psychological volatility and lack of emotional maturity. The most common death that occurs in the teenage years is that of a grandparent, although of course many teenagers experience the death of a parent, sibling, close friend or other relative.

Death and dying is still largely a taboo subject in this country, and one that most people avoid talking about. Teenagers do need to be prepared for the death of those around them, particularly for the death of grandparents and elderly relatives. This does not need to be done in a forced or planned way. It means rather that conversations about death and dying should not be avoided. Talk about it, for example, when a famous person or character in a TV soap dies.

Teenagers should be told if a relative or friend is ill, and that it is possible that they will die. They will then be able to ask questions about the process of dying and death itself. A teenager may also want to say goodbye to a dying person. If they are not prepared in advance for the death of someone close, it will leave them feeling particularly shocked and upset.

When a friend or relative dies, teenagers should be told exactly what happened, and any questions they have should be answered. They should go to the funeral if they want to, but should not be forced to do so.

There are a number of ways parents can help a bereaved teenager. It helps, first, to think about how to talk to teenagers about death, and secondly to understand stages in the grieving process.

Grieving

The process of grieving for someone close can go on for months or even years. Grieving takes many different forms, and can be divided into three stages:

- **Early stage:** immediately following the death of someone close, a teenager may feel shock, numbness, and disbelief.
- **Grieving stage:** young people will normally grieve for the person in the weeks and months following the death. During this stage teenagers may become disorganised, forget important events, and fall behind at school. They may be depressed and frequently upset. They may appear OK for a period of time, and then become very distressed.
- **Coming to terms stage:** here teenagers begin to realise that the loss is final, and that their lives will now be different in some way. They begin to develop a sense that life will continue.

There are a number of things that parents can do to help a teenager who has lost someone close to them. These include the following:

- Giving them time to talk. Make sure you spend some time alone with them, when they can talk about how they feel.
- Talk about *your* feelings about the bereavement, and express your own grief. Let your teenager know it's natural to feel upset, and encourage them to cry if they want to. This is particularly important for boys, who may well feel that they should not express their emotions.
- Let your teenager spend more time with you, or at home, if they want to. Don't encourage them to 'get out more' if they say they are not yet ready.
- Let your teenager's school know – it may help the teenager if their school is aware that his or her work may suffer, or that they may be tearful and upset.

- Talk about the dead person; don't avoid mentioning their name. Remember happy times and good memories.
- Contact a professional organisation if your teenager wants to speak to someone about his or her feelings. The address for CRUSE, who offer counselling and support to people who have been bereaved, is given at the end of the chapter.

Families in Britain today often experience change, whether because of family breakdown or divorce, becoming part of a step-family, or because of the death of a family member. There are of course other events – such as moving home, or a sudden drop in family income because of unemployment – which will also lead to a change in family life. This chapter has suggested some of the ways in which you can help your teenager adapt to the new circumstances they may experience.

Further reading

A useful book which looks at adoption and fostering is by Alison King: *Adoption and fostering – A practical guide*, Crowood, 1989.

The Trust for the Study of Adolescence produces an audio-tape for parents who are divorcing. The tape is called *Teenagers and divorce*. It covers preparing for divorce, sorting out custody and access, managing conflict, and coping with being a lone parent. It is available from TSA Publishing, 23 New Road, Brighton, BN1 1WZ. Tel. 01273-693311.

A useful guide to parenting after divorce is Jill Burrett's *To and fro children*, Thorsons, 1991.

See Fitzhugh Dodson's *How to single parent*, Harper and Row, 1987, which is written mainly for single parents of younger children, but is also useful for single parents of adolescents.

A good book about step-families is *Step-families talking* by Elizabeth Hodder, Optima, 1989.

The Trust for the Study of Adolescence produces an audio-tape and booklet called *Teenagers and step-parents*. The pack deals with envy and jealousy, divided loyalties, and creating a new family. It is available from TSA Publishing, 23 New Road, Brighton, BN1 1WZ. Tel. 0273-693311.

Useful organisations

National Foster Care Association, Leonard House, 5–7 Marshalsea Road, London, SE1 1EP. Tel. 0171-828-6266; 9am–5pm. NFCA provides advice, publications, training materials and videos for all of those involved in fostering.

Gingerbread is an organisation which provides support, help and social activities for lone parents and their children. They also produce publications. Write to: Gingerbread, 49 Wellington Street, London, WC2E 7BN. Tel. 0171-240-0953 for your nearest local organisation..

The **National Council for One Parent Families** provides written information on rights and benefits for single parents. Write to: 255 Kentish Town Road, London, NW5 2LX. Tel. 0171-267-1361.

For general information and advice about step-families contact the **National Step-family Association**, Chapel House, 18 Hatton Place, London, EC1N 8RV. Tel. 0171-209-2460. Helpline 0171-209-2464.

CRUSE – Bereavement Care Tel. 0181-332-7227 9.30am–5pm weekdays.

CHAPTER SIX

Health and health problems

This chapter looks at teenagers' health, and health problems. It covers the following topics:

- Physical health and body image
- Diet and exercise
- Eating disorders
- Smoking and drinking
- Sexual health
- Depression and suicide
- What is 'normal'?
- Getting help

Physical health and body image

Being physically healthy is much more than just not being ill. A healthy adolescent is someone who is able to adjust to the physical changes happening to them, and who has the energy to deal with everyday problems and stresses.

Parents cannot control or constantly monitor their teenagers' physical health. They can, however, provide information and encourage them to have a healthy diet, get sufficient exercise, drink in moderation, and have healthy sexual behaviour.

Each of these areas is addressed in this chapter. The chapter also includes problems relating to physical and psychological health, including eating disorders, depression and suicide. It concludes with advice about where to get help, and a discussion about the difference between 'normal' experimentation and risky behaviour.

Personal hygiene

The bodily changes that occur during puberty mean personal hygiene is important. The hormonal changes that occur at puberty mean that teenagers need to wash and change their clothes regularly. Some young people will do this automatically; others will need prompting and reminding. Remind them that other people may notice a body odour problem, even if they don't.

You may want to help your teenager in other ways, including such things as:

- choosing new products such as sanitary towels or razors;
- selecting and using anti-perspirants and deodorants;
- helping with particular problems such as acne.

Teenagers, especially younger ones, may well feel self-conscious or embarrassed about discussing these things – many of which will be new to them – with parents. Parents can help by opening up conversations, leaving products around for them to look at and try, and by going shopping with them.

Appearance and body image

The onset of puberty makes most teenagers very conscious about their appearance. During adolescence young people will begin to worry about their height, their weight, and their physical characteristics. They will often become preoccupied with one part of their body, and appear overly concerned about problems with their skin or hair.

Teenagers need reassurance about their bodies from their parents. They need to know that they are developing normally, and that they are attractive. In Chapter 1 we described how teenagers often spend a lot of time in the bathroom. This is quite normal. They need time to get used to their new bodies, and to the changes that are happening to them.

Your teenager may change her or his appearance several times during the adolescent years, often in quite dramatic ways. This is because the peer group is very important to young people, and groups of friends often distinguish themselves by their clothes and appearance.

You may think that your teenager's clothes, hair style, make-up or jewellery look absurd. This may be so, but it is important to them and their image, and so it's best just to tolerate it. Adolescence is all about expressing yourself and developing your own identity. Things like clothes and hair style are really not worth arguing with your teenager about – save your efforts for really important issues.

Diet and exercise

In Chapter 2, we described how adolescents' bodies change enormously during adolescence. These changes mean that their bodies have to be properly fed and exercised during this time, which will also help to ensure good health in adulthood. Good diet and exercise are central to this.

Much could be written about the importance of a good diet, and how to promote a good diet amongst teenagers. The essence of a good diet, however, is to:

- eat regularly, including breakfast;
- cut down on fat, sugar and salt;

- increase the intake of fibre;
- eat more fresh fruit and vegetables.

Teenagers' lifestyles often discourage them from doing these things. It's important therefore to encourage your teenager to eat regularly, and to eat less snack and junk foods. It will undoubtedly help if you stress the benefits of healthy eating for a young person's skin and appearance. Young people live for the here and now. Telling them that eating properly will benefit their appearance will undoubtedly strike a chord.

Vegetarian diets

Many teenagers are now choosing to follow vegetarian or vegan diets. Vegetarianism in particular is increasing. Teenagers may give up meat, fish and/or dairy products for moral or ethical reasons, or because they believe it's healthier. For some it may be a temporary change; for others it may last a lifetime.

A vegetarian diet is perfectly healthy, but some extra thought needs to go into what the teenager eats. The following points are particularly important:

- don't simply cut out meat or fish – replace them with foods such as lentils;
- eat more beans, pulses, nuts and cereals to replace lost protein;
- eat more fresh fruit and vegetables.

Buy a few books, or get leaflets for your teenager on vegetarian diets and cooking. There are a large number of these in the shops now. A number of organisations, such as the Vegetarian Society, produce useful publications. These are listed at the end of the chapter.

Obesity

The number of overweight teenagers is rapidly increasing in Britain. Obesity is due to a number of factors, including overeating, eating the wrong sorts of foods, lack of exercise, and a slow metabolism. It is important to support and help a young person who is overweight. It is particularly important not to comment adversely or ridicule an overweight teenager. They are probably already anxious and self-conscious about it.

There are a number of positive things that you can do to help a teenager to lose weight:

- Try to get the whole family to be more food-conscious, eating less fat and more vegetables for example. Don't let the teenager feel that he or she is on a diet, while everyone else is eating normally.
- Don't ban all high calorie or fatty foods. Rather, substitute foods – for example replace full-fat cheese with cottage cheese, or full-cream milk with skimmed milk.
- Limit but don't ban snacks and take-aways. Ensure that these are occasional treats.
- Encourage your adolescent to think long-term. An average weight loss of 1–2 pounds a week is ideal, and at this rate the weight is most likely to stay off. Crash dieting rarely works, and the weight lost is usually put on again quite quickly.
- Encourage your teenager to take more exercise. Remember to start gently and build up. Get other family members involved if you can.
- Plan treats such as an outing or buying new clothes when your teenager reaches certain goals or targets.

Exercise and rest

Study after study has shown that children and young people today weigh more, eat less healthily and get less exercise than teenagers did in previous years. Exercise is central to helping teenagers to become healthier. Try to encourage your teenager to get more exercise and to participate in sports. If they are not keen on team sports, you could suggest cycling, swimming, dancing or walking.

These sports will keep them fit, help to relieve tension, make them feel good about themselves, and may provide new friends.

Feeling healthy also includes getting sufficient rest and sleep. This can be especially difficult when teenagers are starting to go out more. Encourage your teenager to get at least a few early nights in the week.

Eating disorders

There are two main eating disorders which affect adolescents – anorexia nervosa and bulimia. In both cases adolescents become obsessed with the need to lose weight to the point where it totally dominates their lives. Both anorexia and bulimia occur mainly in girls. Boys can, however, also suffer from both illnesses, and about one in five anorexic young people is male.

Anorexia

Anorexia often starts in early adolescence, between the ages of twelve and fifteen, and is particularly prevalent amongst girls. It is a complicated and distressing illness, as the following account from the mother of an anorexic teenager demonstrates:

> *The parents don't really notice any changes . . . It's outsiders that bring it to your attention. That's when you start looking at her. She used to go to the toilet every time she ate something . . . They're really devious. They're up to every trick in the book . . . at the time I don't think we ever realised how serious it was.*

There are a number of signs that suggest a young person may be becoming anorexic:

- an irrational fear of becoming fat;
- severe weight loss;

- a disturbed eating pattern – for example not wanting to eat with people, being secretive about what food they have eaten;
- a disturbed body image, often feeling grossly overweight and repulsive when actually being slim;
- a pale body and a gaunt look;
- being obsessive about exercise;
- denial that eating has become a problem for them.

Anorexia can be extremely damaging to a young person's body, and 15 per cent of anorexics die. Teenagers who are severely anorexic usually have a number of health problems, including low blood pressure, muscle wasting, constipation, hormonal imbalances, and for girls their periods stopping.

The causes of anorexia are unclear. It appears to have a multitude of causes, a number of which may be involved for any particular young person. Factors linked to anorexia in young people include:

- a fear of their developing sexuality;
- a wish to remain a child;
- a feeling of lack of control – food is something a young person can control;
- over-protective and/or over-controlling parents;
- media stereotypes of the ideal body shape.

One young teenager described to us how her anorexia started:

> Your pals and that were all going on a diet and then it just got a hold on me. I just went under weight and that ... I think it just got that much of a grip on me and I could not cope with my body changing. I didn't like myself. I was growing up too fast.

A mother and father that we spoke to talked about their view of the causes of their daughter's anorexia:

> I've always said that anorexics start to lose a pound here and there and it just gets a fix on them. I think

> *they lose half a stone and then they say "my friends are saying I look good, I think I'll lose another half stone". I think it just gets to the stage where they eat so little that they canna begin to eat again.* **?**

Teenagers with anorexia need professional help. Parents cannot, and should not, deal with it themselves. Also, as anorexia is often strongly tied up with the teenager's relationships with their parents, external professional involvement is essential.

The treatment of anorexia can be long and difficult. Most anorexic young people are extremely resistant to any help. Anorexic young people often do not believe – or deny – that there is anything wrong with them, and are totally opposed to the professional's aim of getting them to eat normally.

In cases of extreme weight loss, a teenager with anorexia will need to be hospitalised, at least until she or he has reached a certain weight. After that a course of therapy – often quite long – will be required to help the young person to recognise that they have a problem, and to develop a more realistic body image.

Bulimia

Bulimia is different from anorexia in that instead of not eating, the bulimic binges. After a bout of often excessive and uncontrollable binging, a bulimic induces vomiting. They also often use laxatives and undertake strenuous exercise in an attempt to lose weight and purge the body.

Bulimics are often sociable people who appear well-adjusted. Their binging and vomiting is a secret activity, often undertaken at night and in private. Emotionally, they see-saw from disgust and self-loathing when eating, to elation when they purge themselves.

Bulimia is often more difficult for parents to spot than anorexia, because it may not be accompanied by weight loss. There are, however, a number of warning signs:

- large amounts of food being stored in the teenager's room;

- frequent vomiting or attempts to force vomiting, especially immediately after meals;
- use of laxatives, and sudden bursts of exercising.

As with anorexia, the causes of bulimia are unclear and multi-faceted. Teenagers who suffer from bulimia often feel inadequate, unloved, and depressed. Bulimia is also associated with failed attempts at dieting, where a young person tries to diet, fails, binges to console him or herself, and then induces vomiting in disgust.

Many bulimics manage to keep their problem a secret from parents and friends. If a young person is found to have symptoms of bulimia, again it is important that professional help is sought. Treatment may involve individual therapy, and in most cases a bulimic teenager can be helped to end this damaging activity.

Finally, it is important to note that anorexia and bulimia are not two totally separate problems. A teenager may, for example, be anorexic, but occasionally binge and then purge. Teenagers with the symptoms of either disorder need help. Start off with your GP. The Eating Disorders Association can also offer much advice and support. You will find the address at the end of the chapter.

Smoking and drinking

Young people start to smoke and drink for a number of reasons. They may do it to fit in with their peer group, to be admired, liked and popular. Other reasons include curiosity (to see what it's like), defiance (because they're told not to), and to feel grown up. It is important to understand these reasons, and to acknowledge that most young people will be offered, or try, cigarettes or alcohol during the teenage years. We'll look at smoking and drinking separately below.

Cigarette smoking

Research has consistently shown that young people are not put off cigarette smoking by the shock! horror! facts of what smoking

76

leads to in later life – cancer, heart disease, etc. This all seems a long way off to them. Teenagers live for the here and now, so it is a good idea to work on that – the effects of cigarette smoking on their current physical health and how they look.

If you want to discourage your son or daughter from smoking, make sure that they know that cigarette smoking:

- gives them smelly hair and stained fingernails, bad coughs and yellow teeth;
- makes them more prone to colds and flu, because their lungs become filled with tar;
- is addictive. They can't stop it whenever they want to. Tell them that if they spoke to adult smokers most would say they wished they'd never started;
- may help to keep their weight down. But the differences between smokers and non-smokers are actually very small, and if they do start smoking and then give up, they are very likely to put on weight.

Parents who smoke themselves have a particularly important role to play. Adolescents whose parents smoke are five times more likely to do so themselves. If you can't give up, or don't want to, make sure your son or daughter knows that you are addicted, and point out the effects that cigarettes have had on your health.

Alcohol

Most young people will try alcohol at some point. For many young people, starting to drink is a normal part of growing up. However, alcohol is a drug like any other. It can have serious consequences, and is frequently connected with delinquency, accidents, suicide and having unprotected sex. Parents should and can help their teenager to use alcohol sensibly.

Before your adolescent even tries alcohol, it is worth making sure that they know the facts about it. These include

- alcohol is a drug like any other – you can overdose on it and die;

- alcohol increases risk-taking;
- alcohol is high in calories;
- alcohol intensifies emotions. It may make you happy and relaxed, but it may also make you depressed and anxious;
- people who are drunk are not really much fun to be with;
- alcohol doesn't improve sexual performance. In fact it impairs performance. It also makes teenagers less able to say no to sex, and less likely to use protection if they say yes.

The role of parents in relation to smoking and drinking is a difficult one. However, it is important not to ignore the issues of alcohol or cigarettes, nor refuse to discuss them with your daughter or son. Your teenager will be no doubt be talking about them, and probably trying them, outside the home. You must therefore make some decisions with regard to smoking and drinking.

Some parents tell their teenager that they are not allowed to smoke or drink at all. Others prefer to say that their teenager may try things in moderation only, working on the basis that they are likely to try them anyway. Some parents say that their children may not *smoke*, and impose penalties if they are found to do so, but say that they may drink in moderation. This is something parents have to make their own decisions about. But remember that whatever you say, your son or daughter may well still start drinking and/or smoking, so it's worth trying to open up a dialogue between you about this.

Sexual health

We talked in Chapter 2 about the physical and sexual changes that occur in adolescence.

Two of the most important things you can do to help your teenager to adapt to these changes are:

- talk to your son or daughter about puberty and sexuality, answer their questions honestly, and discuss issues with them;

- prepare them for the changes, give them information, and make literature available.

Talking to young people about sexual development and sexual health is difficult for many parents. Many teenagers too will find talking difficult. It is important, however, and parents need to ensure that their teenager is getting accurate information and advice from at least one source, whether from you, their school, or an advice centre.

Sexual health is a very broad topic. It is more than just ensuring that a sexually active young person uses protection. It includes things like:

- having the personal skills to resist the pressure to have sex before the teenager is ready;
- knowing the facts about fertility and contraception;
- feeling happy with their sexual orientation.

Three of the areas central to sexual health are contraception, pregnancy, and sexual orientation. These are discussed in turn below.

Contraception

Many parents say that they would like their children to delay their first sexual experience until they are sixteen, eighteen or later. This is of course very difficult for parents, as they cannot actually prevent their son or daughter from having a sexual relationship. Regardless of their parents' views and advice on the matter, some young people will have a sexual relationship in their teenage years. A recent survey found that the average age of first sexual intercourse was seventeen.

It is therefore vital that all young people are aware of the facts before they become sexually active. Research shows that providing young people with information about sex does not encourage them to become sexually active. The evidence actually suggests the opposite – that providing young people with information and giving them space to talk about relationships and sex generally leads them to delay their first sexual experience. They're also more likely to use contraception when they do have sex. Most young people agree with this, saying that they would like to be able to talk about these issues. One young woman explained how she wanted support and advice from her parents about sexual relationships and contraception:

> *I think parents should understand things like that and not say "if I find out you're doing this ..." If I'd been going out with somebody for say a month, I would really find it nice if they would say "would you like to come with me to the doctor, we'll see about putting you on the pill". I'd really appreciate that. It would make me feel a lot more moral.*

It is particularly important that teenagers know about the need for contraception before they start to have a sexual relationship. They also need to know about the facts of fertility; many young people, for example, are unaware of the times of the month that women are most fertile. They need to have access to contraceptive advice and products, whether from their GP, family planning clinic, or youth advice centre. Teenagers should be told about the morning after pill, which prevents the fertilised ovum from developing. It must be administered within 72 hours of sexual intercourse.

If a parent feels unable to discuss any or all of these topics with a teenager, then they should ensure that someone else does, whether it's a teacher, someone involved in the school sex education programme, aunt, uncle, or cousin.

Pregnancy

An unplanned pregnancy during the teenage years can be devastating for a young person. If your daughter does get pregnant, however, it is vitally important that you offer support and understanding no matter how angry or upset you are. The decision about whether to continue with a pregnancy or to have an abortion is a difficult one, and a young woman will need good advice and the opportunity to talk about her feelings. The teenager must, in the end, feel she has made a decision to which she is committed.

Of course the young man involved should be included in the discussions about what to do. He must be encouraged to see the fact that the girl is pregnant as their joint responsibility. Parents of girls who get pregnant will no doubt be angry, and may want to exclude the boy from the decision-making process. Both the boy and the girl, however, should be involved in the discussion if at all possible.

Teenagers and their parents do not have to go through an unplanned pregnancy alone. There are many organisations which provide information and can help with the emotional and practical sides of a teenage pregnancy, including the British Pregnancy Advice Centre and the Brook Advisory Centre. Their addresses are at the end of this chapter.

Sexual orientation

It is important for teenagers to develop a real sense of who they are in adolescence. Feeling happy with your sexual orientation is central to sexual health.

Most young people develop a heterosexual orientation in adolescence. Others will have a strong attachment to people of the same sex. This may be temporary, or it may not. Some young people will develop a permanent lesbian or gay sexual orientation.

Many studies have shown that a large proportion of homosexual adults knew they were lesbian or gay early on in their lives, often during adolescence. Some young people don't 'come out' until after the teenage years, anxious about the reaction from parents and friends. Some never feel able to come out at all. For many parents, the disclosure (or discovery) that their teenager is gay or lesbian can be confusing and distressing.

It is important that gay and lesbian young people are accepted for who they are, and supported in coming to terms with their sexual identity. There are a number of organisations which give help and advice to gay and lesbian young people, and to their families, such as Acceptance. These organisations are listed at the end of this chapter.

Depression and suicide

In Chapters 1 and 2, we talked about the volatile nature of adolescents – happy and excitable one day, sad and irritable the next. Most adolescents will therefore show some depressive symptoms during the teenage years, especially after difficult events such as failing an exam, or the ending of a relationship. Parents need to be supportive at these times, allowing young people to talk about how they feel. Parents also need to help young people to see that the event is not the end of the world, and that they can move on from it.

Some adolescents, however, do experience more serious signs of stress and bouts of depression. For some, it may follow a traumatic event – the death of a parent, or parental separation. For others, it may appear to have developed over time and have no apparent cause.

Signs of depression

There are a number of warning signs that an adolescent is suffering from stress, and/or depression:

- loss of appetite and weight;
- lack of concentration and decline in school performance;
- neglect of personal hygiene and appearance;
- withdrawal from friends and usual activities;
- disturbed sleep or insomnia;
- persistently feeling 'down';

- feeling that life isn't worth living, suicidal thoughts and comments.

Sometimes a young person may just have one of these symptoms. The key to recognising true depression is:

- the combination of a number of these symptoms;
- the persistence of these problems over a length of time;
- the effect these problems have on the adolescent's ability to lead a normal daily life.

You cannot get out of it. It's just there, like a cage round you. It's like somebody's thrown the key away.

Help for teenagers with depression

A young person who is depressed needs help and support from their parents and family, as well as professional help. Their problems should not be ignored, nor should they be told to 'pull themselves together' or to 'snap out of it'. Depression makes young people very low in self-worth, and the implication that they are not trying to help themselves can make the situation worse. Teenagers need to know that their parents care, and that they want to help.

Involving your GP can be the best place to start if your teenager seems to be seriously depressed. This can be difficult, however, as many teenagers will deny that they are depressed, or reject help because of embarrassment or a feeling that no one will understand them. Teenagers who are depressed need to know that many people experience depression, and that they can be helped. Research shows that teenagers are more likely to talk about their symptoms and feelings to a sympathetic detached outsider. Your GP may well therefore be the best first port of call. Other organisations can help – many of these are listed at the end of this chapter.

Treatment for teenage depression can include anti-depressant drugs, individual or group therapy. Different treatments will work best for different young people. It is important for your teenager to know what is happening, and to have people to talk to about it. Parents, too, will need help – some useful books and organisations are listed at the end of the chapter and may help to provide support and information to parents.

Suicide

Suicide is sometimes associated with depression. A suicidal young person, or a young person who does take their own life, can be one of the hardest experiences for parents and families to cope with. Recent figures show that suicide and attempted suicide are increasing amongst young people, and in particular amongst boys and young men.

There are a number of warning signs that a young person may be suicidal:

- a persistant sense of hopelessness;
- problems sleeping and lack of appetite;
- loss of interest in school and outide activities;
- talking about suicide or being dead;
- withdrawal from family and friends;
- self-harming acts, for example cutting themselves.

A young person who talks about or threatens suicide needs help. It is completely untrue that those who talk about suicide don't ever attempt it. Parents need help to deal with a suicidal teenager. Contact your GP, or the Samaritans for advice. Don't just ignore it or hope that it will go away.

When a teenager attempts suicide, parents most commonly feel disbelief and then anger. Difficult as it can be at the time, your teenager needs your understanding, help and support. You need to know what made them so distressed that they could think about killing themselves – listen to what they have to say. Young people may attempt suicide in response to a one-off event, or as a way of dealing with an intolerable situation. You need to know about your son or daughter's problems in order to help them.

What is 'normal'?

In chapters 1 and 2, we discussed the fact that the teenage years are a time of experimentation, testing of boundaries, and the development of individual identities. This means that most teenagers want to try new experiences.

There will also be encouragement from your teenager's peer group to try out new things. These experiences may include – as we have shown in this chapter – smoking cigarettes or trying alcohol, wearing distinctive clothes or make-up, or having sex. In all these areas it is necessary to distinguish natural curiosity and experimentation which is relatively safe (for example trying a cigarette or attempting to lose a few pounds), with risky and unsafe behaviours (such as having unprotected sex, dieting to excess, or regular heavy drinking). Teenagers need to have some boundaries in all of these areas, and to be protected from risky behaviour. Guidance from parents, as we have said, is essential.

The next chapter talks further about some of these activities, and about how parents can help young people protect themselves from risk.

Getting help

Throughout this chapter, we have talked about situations where teenagers may need professional help. Getting help for a son or daughter can be daunting for many parents. It is often difficult to know where to go for advice. Some parents may also lack the confidence to look for help. It is, however, important for parents to seek out help if they have a problem with their teenager that they feel they cannot handle. Parents, too, will need the help and support that outside organisations can give. Here's what one mother said about getting help for her teenage daughter:

> Phone the Samaritans, phone a Parents Helpline, phone the vicar ... speak to anybody that could possibly put you onto somebody who can help with even part of the problem. But do it early. Don't try and muddle through on your own.

Knowing where to start in looking for help can be difficult. For many parents, the GP will be the first person to talk to. Your GP will also be able to suggest more specialist help.

There are also now a number of voluntary and self-help groups which can be helpful – there are groups which help parents of teenagers with eating disorders, or teenagers who are being bullied for example. Most of these groups were founded by parents who had a problem themselves, and felt that they had nowhere to go. These organisations are there to help parents and teenagers who are in difficulty. Don't be afraid to use them.

Many professional and voluntary organisations are listed at the end of this chapter and throughout the book. If they don't have the information that you want or cannot help, look elsewhere. It can be frustrating to find telephone numbers constantly engaged, or to speak to an organisation that doesn't have the information you want. But it's important to keep trying. Information and addresses of organisations can be found in such places as:

- local libraries;
- Citizen's Advice Bureaux;
- schools;
- community health councils and local hospitals.

'Hanging on in there'

If a teenager is involved in crime, is depressed, or has an eating disorder, it will inevitably be distressing and draining for parents. Often the situation may feel hopeless. However, a number of the parents and young people that we spoke to talked about the importance of 'hanging on in there'. We'll finish this chapter with two parents whose children had problems:

> *There's no reason why, because you think yours is the worst, that he really is the worst. He probably isn't. Stick around. He's an OK person.*

> *I'd say to parents they're not doing it to you. It's not for you. You may never find out who they're doing it to, but stop persecuting yourself*

Finally, here is a teenager who had a major drug problem, talking about her parents who stuck by her when she was in difficulty:

> *It's been sort of like "we want to help you", because, I'm not being vain, because they think I'm worth helping. I'm their daughter. That's really helped me. I think that kind of attitude is really nice.*

Further reading

The **Health Education Authority** publishes a large amount of information on most health topics. Most of this is available free, and includes information for teenagers. Contact them at HEA, Hamilton House, Mabledon Place, London, WC1H 9TX. Tel. 0171-383-3833.

Getting physical – A teenage health guide by Aric Signan (BBC Books, 1992) is a book for young people, with sections on food, weight and body shape, hygeine, and emotions.

A useful book on eating disorders with sections on bulimia, anorexia, obesity, and getting help for those with eating disorders is *Eating disorders*, Mike Smith, Kyle Cathie, 1994.

HEALTH AND HEALTH PROBLEMS

The Trust for the Study of Adolescence produces a pack called *Teenagers and Alcohol*. It considers the issues of peer pressure, dealing with alcohol in social situations, drinking and driving, alcohol and crime, and alcoholism in the family. Available from TSA Publishing, 23 New Road, Brighton, BN1 1WZ. Tel. 01273-693311.

For a look at all areas of stress for young people, see *Teenage stress* by Charmaine Saunders, Milner, 1992.

An excellent book on teenagers' problems is called *Young people under stress: A parents' guide*, by Sally Burningham, Virago, 1994. It includes a good section on where to go for help and the sorts of treatments available.

Useful organisations

For general information about vegetarian diets contact the **Vegetarian Society**, Parkdale, Dunham Road, Altrincham, Cheshire, WA14 4QG. Tel. 0161-928-0793.

For information and advice about anorexia, bulimia, and compulsive overeating contact the **Eating Disorders Association**, at Sackville Place, 44–48 Magdalen Street, Norwich, Norfolk, NR3 1JU. Tel. 01603-621414. Parents and young people can phone the helpline, which is open 9am–6.30pm weekdays. A youth helpline is open on Mondays, Tuesdays and Wednesdays from 4–6pm on 01603-765050.

88

Contact **QUIT** for help and advice for smokers who want to quit. Its Quitline, staffed by trained counsellors, is open 9am–11pm every day. Tel. 0171-487-3000. It also produces a free pack on giving up smoking for sixteen- to nineteen-year-olds.

Al-Anon Family Groups provide a 24-hour confidential helpline for people and families affected by drinkers. **Alateen** provides the same service for young people between the ages of twelve and twenty. Both can be contacted at 61 Great Dover Street, London, SE1 4YF. Tel 0171-403-0888.

For advice on pregnancy, abortion and contraception contact the **British Pregnancy Advice Service** at 7 Belgrave Road, London, SW1V 1QB. Tel. 0171-828-2484.

The **Brook Advisory Centre** provides contraceptive advice and counselling for teenagers and young people. It is free and confidential. For your nearest centre contact Brook at 165 Grays Inn Road, London, WC1X 8UD. Tel. 0171-713-9000. There are regional centres around the country.

A helpline is available for parents of gay and lesbian young people. Contact **Acceptance** at 64 Holmside Avenue, Halfway Houses, Sheerness, Kent ME12 3EY. Tel. 01795-661463, 7–9pm Tuesday to Friday. They can sometimes be contacted during the day. Acceptance also produces a newsletter, and has some local groups.

MIND, the mental health charity, can offer support and advice for people with a mental health problem. Contact MIND at Granta House, 15–19 Broadway, Stratford, London E15 4BQ. Tel. 0181-519-2122.

HEALTH AND HEALTH PROBLEMS

Young Minds campaigns to raise public awareness of, and to improve, mental health services and resources for children and young people. Telephone or write to them for information on national and local services at Young Minds, 22a Boston Place, London, NW1 6ER. Tel. 0171-724-7262.

CHAPTER SEVEN

Risk-taking

This chapter looks at the following areas, which all concern teenagers and risk:

- Living close to the edge
- Crime and delinquency
- Substances: drugs and solvents
- Sexual risk
- Keeping safe inside and outside the home

Living close to the edge

Experimenting and taking certain risks is a normal part of adolescent development. Some teenagers, however, take considerable risks. Such risks may damage their health and futures, and can endanger their lives. This chapter deals with some of the most common risks that teenagers take – getting involved in crime, substance use and abuse, and sexual risk – and suggests ways in which you can help your teenager to remain safe. Finally, the chapter looks at teenagers' personal safety in and out of the home.

RISK-TAKING

There are a number of risks for adolescents which particularly concern parents. The sorts of things that parents mentioned to us were:

- having a road accident;
- being sexually assaulted/raped;
- getting a girl pregnant/getting pregnant;
- dropping out of school;
- getting involved in crime;
- using drugs.

Taking risks is not limited to teenagers. It is also not new. Parents may want to think about the risks that they took – bouts of drinking, using a motorbike, having unprotected sex. It is worth acknowledging the difficulty most of us have in recognising or accepting the risks we take in our lives. This is especially true for young people.

However, parents can help teenagers to reduce risks. In Chapter 2, we discussed the importance of establishing good communication between parents and teenagers. We talked about setting boundaries and guidelines with teenagers, and about negotiation and agreement.

These strategies are essential if parents are to steer teenagers away from taking excessive risks. Listening, discussing, explaining, and negotiating are all crucial to the process. Also, if ground rules and guidelines are provided, then teenagers will know that parents will intervene if a situation gets out of hand. Simply laying down the law is unlikely to steer teenagers away from risky behaviour.

Deciding when a situation is dangerous enough for parents to intervene is a difficult one. In the long-term, parents want their teenager to manage his or her own life. There are clearly times, however, when you have to seek help for your daughter or son – for example if they become addicted to alcohol or drugs, or if they become anorexic. Sometimes parents may be uncertain about whether the problem is serious or not. If you have any doubts, do not be afraid to ask for professional advice.

Crime and delinquency

Research has shown that most young people break the law in some way during the adolescent years. Most of us can probably think of things that we did as teenagers, which may have involved theft or vandalism. For most young people, though, activities such as stealing from a shop happen only once or twice, or for a short period.

Some young people, however, become locked in a cycle of crime and law-breaking. This is most common amongst boys, although girls are also sometimes involved. For this group, offending often starts at a young age – the peak age for offending is fifteen for boys and fourteen for girls. Most research shows that juvenile offenders are characterised by:

- poor attendance/attainment at school;
- family poverty and unemployment;
- peer group offending behaviour;
- poor or inconsistent parental supervision;
- a sibling or parent involved in offending.

A recurring theme in studies of teenage offenders is that many of these young people have difficulty in dealing with authority and authority figures. Their reaction to people in authority – such as parents, teachers, and the police – is often aggression, conflict, and sometimes violence.

Teenagers need to learn to live with authority. In Chapter 2 we discussed how certain styles and methods of parenting can help to reduce the potential for disagreement and conflict within the family. In Chapter 4 we talked about how to minimise the effect of peer group encouragment to become involved in offending. These strategies will not guarantee that your son or daughter does not get involved with crime. However, they are likely to help to prevent it.

Strategies for parents to use include the following:

- Show love and affection. Young people need to know that their parents love them. These bonds are likely to increase the influence parents have over children.
- Set boundaries and rules. Don't just let young people 'do their own thing'. They need to know the rules. More importantly perhaps they need to know that these rules are there not for petty reasons, but to protect them and keep them safe. Young people also need to be clear about – and have agreed – the penalties incurred in breaking the rules.
- Use negotiation and agreement. Discuss things with your teenager, and give reasons for your decisions. Involve the adolescent in the decision-making process.
- Be consistent. Young people need to be clear where they stand. Don't change the rules or the punishments in an arbitrary way.
- Increase responsibility over a period of time. As your teenager grows, give them more responsibility for their lives and decisions.
- Show that you disapprove of any involvement they have in criminal or delinquent acts.

Parents of teenagers involved in crime often feel guilty and responsible, and feel that they've failed in some way. Neverthless, whatever a young person has done, they still need to feel loved and supported. However difficult it is at the time, it is important to remember that research shows that by their early twenties many of those who have been in trouble as teenagers have stopped offending.

Substances: drugs and solvents

In Chapter 5, we introduced the topic of drugs by talking about the two most commonly used drugs by teenagers and adults – cigarettes and alcohol. We suggested that parents had to decide what line they wanted to take with their teenagers on both of these substances.This section looks at the issues around other types of drugs, and solvents.

Many young people today will be offered, and some will use, drugs such as cannabis, ecstasy, and LSD, and solvents such as glue, cleaning fluids, and petrol. These substances have different effects on young people's physical and psychological health. It is important to know the facts about the different drugs available, and their effects on teenagers. The help and advice organisations listed at the end of this chapter can give you accurate and up-to-date information about all types of drugs.

Most parents fear that their teenager will start to use drugs or solvents. Indeed, research has consistently shown that teenagers today are likely to be offered drugs, and many will go on to try them.

It is important for parents to get information for themselves and their teenager, and to talk to their son or daughter about drugs and solvents. Talking to a teenager who seems ignorant of the facts will not make them want to experiment with drugs. It will, however, enable them to make sensible decisions if and when they do come into contact with drugs.

Signs of drug use

There are a number of signs that a teenager may regularly be using drugs. These include

- mood swings;
- lack of interest in friends or usual activities;
- difficulty in concentrating;
- tiredness;
- secretiveness;
- loss of appetite;
- money missing from the home.

A teenager could of course have one or more of these symptoms and still not be using drugs. So it is important for parents to tread carefully, and find out the facts.

If a teenager is found to be using drugs, their parents' immediate reaction may be to show their anger. Your teenager needs to know, however, that you are angry or upset because of the damage drugs and solvents have on their health, safety and future prospects. They need to know that you want to help them.

How you can help

There are a number of things you can do if your son or daughter is taking drugs or using solvents:

- Contact your GP or a professional organisation for help and advice. You need to know the facts.
- Talk to your daughter or son. What exactly have they been using? Do they use it occasionally, or regularly? Why do they do it? How does it make them feel? Do they understand the risks? Do they want to stop?
- Be patient – it may take several sessions to find out the answers to these questions. If they clam up, enlist their brothers or sisters, or a family friend.
- Do they know the dangers? Talk with them about the risks. For most drugs and solvents the effects include:
    risk of overdose and death;
    addiction;
    long-term physical and mental impairment;
    doing dangerous acts when on a 'high';
    infections like hepatitus or HIV/AIDS if drugs are injected.
- Agree a plan of action with them. Talk through the reasons they take the drug. Is it because their friends do, for excitement, because they're fed up?

Drug and substance use is one of the most difficult areas for parents to deal with. It is important for parents not to take all the pressure themselves. Speak to friends, your teenager's school, teachers, your GP, or professional organisations. A number of these organisations are listed at the end of this chapter. With the right help, your teenager can come off and stay off drugs and solvents.

Sexual risk

In Chapter 6, we talked about your teenager's sexual *health*. Sexual *risk* is closely tied to the topics we talked about there. Risk includes being pressurised into sex, and having unprotected sex. Sexual activity without protection is always risky. It can lead to pregnancy and increases the risk of the transmission of sexually transmitted diseases, particularly HIV/AIDS. A crucial component of sex education, whether by parents or schools, must therefore be a focus on the risks of unplanned sexual activity.

Research has shown that many girls who become pregnant as teenagers lacked the information necessary to prevent pregnancy. Indeed, current research evidence suggests that 50 per cent of adolescents used no contraception the first time they had sex. The reasons teenagers give for not using contraception include:

- they were drunk;
- they didn't have any contraception;
- they felt embarrassed to ask the girl/boy about it.

It is important that you talk to your teenager about such possibilities. Being prepared for unexpected or new situations is a crucial part of sexual health.

Another situation for which your teenager needs to be prepared – particularly if she is a girl – is that of sexual coercion or violence. Teenagers need to know that they can say no to sex for whatever reason. They should know how to say no unambiguously and assertively. They also need to know that being drunk can affect their willingness or ability to say no.

Parents must help young people to anticipate difficult situations, so that they can ensure their own safety. These can be difficult subjects to talk to teenagers about, but parents need to help young people to be aware of the issues and risks. There are a number of ways to start conversations about these topics. These include:

- Talk about items in the newspaper or on the radio. These might be about a teenager becoming pregnant, or about a rape case. Discuss the issues with them, what they would do, how they feel.
- Use TV soaps as springboards for discussion. Most soaps contain incidents of unplanned sexual activity. Again, get your teenager to think about what they would do in particular circumstances, and about how risks can be reduced in different situations.
- Talk about people you know, and dilemmas or issues facing them. Help your teenager to understand that everyone is placed in a risky situation at some point, and that they should think about how they might act beforehand.

Keeping safe in and out of the home

Young children spend most of their time with their parents. In adolescence, young people spend much more time on their own or with friends, in the house and outside. Most teenagers will find themselves in a risky situation at some point during adolescence. They need to be prepared for these events, without making them feel anxious. Teenagers need guidance from their parents about how to stay safe inside and outside the home.

Inside the home

When teenagers are in the family home, a number of things are important:

- If your son or daughter is alone in the house, make sure they know never to let anyone in without being absolutely certain who they are.
- Make sure they have the telephone number of a friend or neighbour, whom they can contact if they have a problem.
- If they have a new friend round, talk to this person. How did your son or daughter meet them, where do they live?

Outside the home

Talk with your teenager about risks outside the home. In particular, stress the following:

- Avoid dark and deserted places.
- Never accept a lift from a stranger.
- Never hitch-hike.
- If someone is following them, or is harrassing them, they should go into a shop or house, or ask a passer-by for help.
- If they are out late and have missed a bus or a lift from friends, tell them to phone you to pick them up, or get a taxi. Make sure they know never to walk home alone at night. Ensure that they always have change for a telephone, or a telephone card, and some emergency money.
- Tell them not to carry weapons. It is illegal to carry many weapons, and in most cases a person's weapon is used against them. Some teenagers feel safer if they have a rape alarm; talk to your son or daughter about whether they would like one.
- Many girls in particular now take self-defence courses. Try to find a course for your teenager if they want to go on one. Most courses start off by talking about risk, and how to avoid dangerous or risky situations. Only then do they move on to physical self-defence.

You cannot protect your teenager from every dangerous or risky event that might happen as they grow up. However, you can help them to anticipate the things that might happen to them, and think about how they can protect themselves. This chapter has suggested a number of ways that this can be done. The books and organisations listed at the end of the chapter can provide more information about reducing risks in particular areas. They can also help if your teenager is already in trouble in some way. These organisations are there to help – use them.

Further reading

A good book, which includes sections on harrassment, safety on the streets, rape, and self-defence, is *Safe, Strong and Streetwise* by Helen Benedict, Hodder and Stoughton, 1987.

Teenagers involved in crime and delinquency are discussed in *Teenagers under stress*, a pack produced by the Trust for the Study of Adolescence. This pack also looks at alcohol, drugs, leaving home, depression, and sexuality. Contact TSA Publishing, 23 New Road, Brighton, East Sussex, BN1 1WZ. Tel. 01273-693311.

The Trust for the Study of Adolescence produces a pack called *Teenagers and drugs*. The audio-tape and booklet looks at the range of drugs available, how to recognise signs of abuse, the type of support available and where to get help and advice. Available from TSA Publishing, 23 New Road, Brighton, East Sussex, BN1 1WZ. Tel. 01273-693311.

Useful organisations

Drugline Dial 100 and ask for 'Freephone Drug Problems'. You will hear a recorded message about services in your county.

For information on drugs and solvents contact **Release**. It provides a 24-hour emergency helpline on 0171-603-8654. Or write to 388 Old Street, London, EC1V 9LT. Tel. 0171-729-9904 Mon–Fri 10am–6pm for advice.

Adfam National is a national charity for the families and friends of drug users. Its National helpline can be contacted on 0171-638-3700 Mon–Fri 10am–5pm. Or write to Adfam, 5th floor, Epworth House, 25 City Road, London, EC1Y 1AA.

For information and advice about HIV/AIDS contact **National Aids Helpline**. Tel. 0800-567123 (FREE).

The **Brook Advisory Centre** provides contraceptive advice and counselling to teenagers and young people. It is free and confidential. For your nearest centre contact: Central Office, Brook Advisory Centre, 165 Grays Inn Road, London, WC1X 8UD. Tel. 0171-713-9000.

CHAPTER EIGHT

Schools and beyond

This chapter looks at issues to do with teenagers and schools, and planning for the future. It includes:

- Secondary schools, teenagers, and parents
- Homework
- Coping with exams
- Part-time work while at school
- Planning for the future
- School refusal and truancy
- Teenagers with special needs

Secondary schools, teenagers and parents

Young people spend a considerable amount of their teenage years in school. For most young people, it's the centre of their world. School is where their friends are, where they learn and develop skills and interests, and where they prepare and plan for the future.

Some teenagers enjoy their school years very much. Others have difficult and distressing experiences. Most young people have a mixture of good and bad times. Parents have a vital role to play in helping their teenager enjoy their school years.

This chapter talks about the main issues involved in education and in planning for the future – homework and exams, part-time work while at school, school refusal and truancy, and helping teenagers with special needs.

The move to secondary school

A key change for most young people early on in the teenage years is the move to a secondary school. At primary level children are usually at a small school, with one teacher for the year. Secondary schools are usually much larger, and teenagers will have a different teacher for each subject. The change also represents a move from being the oldest at primary school to becoming the newest and youngest member of the school. It's hardly surprising therefore that many young people feel anxious about the move to secondary school.

You can help to smooth the transfer from primary to secondary school in a number of ways. These include:

- Talking to your son or daughter about the differences between primary and secondary school. Feeling prepared can make all the difference in adjusting to a major change.
- Focusing on the good things about the new school – being at a 'grown-up' school, the better sporting or music facilities, having more clubs and out of school activities.
- Trying to ensure that your son or daughter has someone to go with on the first day, perhaps a friend or someone from the local area. This will give them confidence and help them feel less isolated.
- Making sure that they feel able to talk to you if they have any problems at the new school.

The relationship between you and your teenager's school is likely to be quite different as your child moves from primary to secondary school. Many parents know their child's teacher at primary school, and have many informal contacts with the school. At secondary level this changes. Most teenagers will make their own way to school, and there are unlikely to be the informal meetings with teachers or other parents at the school gate.

You may therefore feel rather distant or alienated from your teenager's school. You may not know who to talk to for information or advice. Some parents may lack the confidence to approach someone at the school. This is particularly true for parents who have had a bad experience of schooling themselves, or who feel they lack the skills or knowledge to discuss personal and educational matters with teachers and professionals.

Parents who are knowledgeable and involved in their son's or daughter's school are in the best position to help and advise their teenagers. Most schools want, and encourage, good relationships with parents. They know that good school–home contact contributes both to young people's learning and behaviour.

Getting involved with your teenager's school

Most schools are becoming much more parent friendly. There are a number of different ways that parents can get involved with their teenager's school. These include:

- Attending parents' evenings and open days.
- Getting involved in the PTA (Parent Teacher Association), or Parents Association (PA) as they're becoming increasingly known. PTAs have regular meetings, and discuss a wide range of issues concerning the school, such as staffing or the curriculum.
- Reading the newsletters and information that is produced by the school. Telephone or write to the school with any questions or concerns.

- Volunteering to work in the school – helping with sports, in the library, accompanying school trips, etc.

It is good for all concerned when teenagers, parents and schools are in close contact. This can of course be difficult, especially as many parents will be working when their teenager's school is open. Getting involved in the activities listed above will help though. If you feel awkward or uncertain, why not try to get another parent to get more involved with you? Being involved in the school will help parents make their teenager's education more enjoyable and rewarding.

Homework

The amount of homework young people are given increases steadily throughout the secondary school years, in particular because many GCSE courses now have large amounts of coursework which is assessed. It is important for parents to show an interest in their teenagers homework. However, this does not mean that parents should be tempted to do their daughter or son's homework for them. Your teenager may become dependent on you doing the work for them, and your knowledge may be wrong or out of date. Offer help and support by making sure that they do the work.

There are a number of constructive ways to help teenagers with their homework:

- Be interested – ask about your teenager's homework, what subjects they're doing, what special projects they have.
- Make physical space for your teenager to do their homework – find an area in the house where they can work undisturbed.
- Help your son or daughter to structure their time, so that they have a regular homework slot. It may be straight after school, early evening, or even early each morning.

- Help them to locate resources and information – for example finding an atlas at a local library.
- If they really cannot do the homework they've been given, make sure they feel able to tell the teacher concerned.

Coping with exams

6 ... it's all very well telling me to try not to worry too much. You just remember that this is the whole of the rest of my life we're talking about. 9

Exams make most young people – like most adults – very anxious. This is of course quite normal. Most people manage to get through the exam despite this nervousness. For a small number of young people, however, their anxiety is so great that they cannot function properly in the exam. These young people may need extra help.

6 I think the exams are very stressful. I broke down and cried last week. My parents just kept saying "Oh what's wrong with you, you're so moody" and they didn't seem to understand that I'd just taken my A Levels and that if I failed them what were they going to do. I did sit down and cry. 9

There are a number of things that parents can do to help young people through the stress of revision and exams:

- Help them to structure their revision time so that they pace themselves. Encourage them to study and revise over the weeks or months before the exam, and not the day or night before.
- Encourage them to have some time off the evening before an exam: suggest they stop revising, take a long walk, and get a good night's sleep.

- Talk about exam technique with them, including:
    reading the questions thoroughly before starting to write;
    answering the question – not just recounting what they've
    revised;
    dividing the time between the different questions;
    leaving time to read the answers through at the end.
- Some young people find it helpful to look at a book on
  study skills.
- Remind them that you love and value them, and whatever
  happens in the exam won't alter that.

Part-time work while at school

Many young people now have a Saturday, Sunday or evening job
whilst they are at school. Most do it, of course, to earn extra
money. Many need to work to help with the family's finances. A
few young people may be pursuing a particular interest or trying to
get work experience for the future.

Working has many benefits for teenagers. For example part-time
work:

- provides extra funds;
- develops money sense and responsibility;
- promotes organisation and discipline;
- provides new friends;
- gives experience of the world of work.

There are also, however, a number of disadvantages to
teenagers working. These might include:

- long hours and tiredness;
- having less time for homework;
- spending less time with parents – missing meals and family
  excursions for example – and so becoming more distant
  from parents;
- jobs which can be dangerous.

Balancing work and play

Parents need to accept that most young people want to work at some point while they're at school. This being so, teenagers need to get a balance between part-time work and the other aspects of their lives.

Parents can help teenagers to get this balance right in a number of ways. You can:

- talk about the disadvantages of working – missing social events and trips, extra-curricular activities;
- talk about money management. Suggest they set up an account and regularly save some of the money;
- talk about what hours they could work. Too many hours or working late in the evening may make them tired. Agree a maximum number with them;
- discuss whether they should work in the evenings or at weekends only;
- discuss how they will get to and from work. Are they expecting a parent to help them with transport?
- agree to review the effect the work is having on their life a few weeks after they start. Is their school work suffering? Are they missing out on social or extra-curricular activities?

It is important for teenagers to think ahead about working part-time. Parents should discuss with them the need to get a balance between their current needs and their future needs and ambitions.

Planning for the future

During the teenage years, schools and parents want to help children to reach their full potential, and to gain experiences and qualifications that will enable them to get fulfilling jobs and enrich their lives.

❝ *It's also more stressful than parents realise, having to decide what you're going to do with your life. It's such a big decision and it really wears you down . . . Oh it's terrible. You need as much help as you can and as many options given to you as possible.* ❞

There are a number of ways that parents can help their teenager to plan for the future. These things will of course be different at different ages. It may be useful to think in terms of the early and late teenage years:

Early teens (age twelve to fourteen)

- Encourage your teenager to think about the future. What are they interested in? What are they good at?
- Encourage them to choose their GCSE subjects carefully. Which will give them the most options in the future? Which subjects have more coursework or more exams, and which would they prefer?
- Stress the link between working hard at school now, and doing something they want to do in the future, such as going to university or getting a particular job.
- Talk to your teenager's teachers. What are your child's best subjects? Where do their skills and interests lie?

Late teens (age fifteen to eighteen)

- Start planning and making decisions with your teenager – do they want to stay on in education, or leave school at sixteen? What education, training and work opportunities are there for them?
- Encourage them to get some work experience. Most schools organise work experience at this point. If there isn't

any organised by the school or in an area that your teenager wants, help them to organise some for themselves.
- Make sure they keep their options as open as possible, by not specialising too early. Remind them that they may make one decision but change their mind later on. For example, if at age sixteen they say they want to be a pharmacist, remind them they may want to do something else by age eighteen. Make sure they don't close off too many options too early.
- Stress that other experiences and extra-curricular activities are important – sport, music, and voluntary service for example. These activities will make them much more rounded individuals, and will also appeal to interviewers when they are applying for courses and jobs.

Your teenager's school will, of course, be closely involved with your son or daughter's future plans. Most schools now put considerable effort and resources into careers planning. There will be someone at the school who is responsible for careers information and advice. Teenagers should be encouraged to contact them if they lack information or are unsure what to do. Parents may also want to meet the careers staff.

Unemployment

Short periods or longer spells of unemployment are now real possibilities for many young people after they have left school. The risk of unemployment varies considerably throughout the country, and between different sectors of the population. Northern Ireland, the north-east and south Wales have particularly high rates of unemployment. In addition, many more black teenagers than white teenagers are unemployed. Less than one in ten young people now goes straight into a job at the age of 16. Some stay on in full-time or part-time education, others go onto training schemes.

Those teenagers who experience unemployment face a difficult time. Many become demoralised and depressed, and many live in poverty. Most unemployed young people spend increasing amounts of time at home. This can cause problems. The risk of rows and arguments increases. Whilst parents cannot usually provide their son or daughter with work, you can help your teenager in a number of ways:

- not blaming them for their situation;
- offering support and hope, making sure they know that you are with them and have confidence that they will find something eventually;
- helping them to structure their day. Encourage them to get involved in sports, voluntary work, and hobbies;
- supporting their job-seeking activities, such as following up personal contacts, and helping them with their job applications;
- talking to them about training opportunities. You could visit the local Careers Office and speak to local colleges.

School refusal and truancy

School refusal and truancy are two quite different things, with very different causes. Both, however, involve young people not attending their school regularly. We'll look first at school refusal.

School refusal

There are a number of signs of school refusal. A teenager may:

- complain of illness each morning;
- be distressed in the morning, saying that they don't want to go to school;
- leave school early.

As one mother of a school refuser told us:

SCHOOLS AND BEYOND

> *Well I suppose it was obvious really . . . he just refused to go. He was I think about ten. It creeps up. It's not noticeable at first because usually . . . he would be ill. He would have psychosomatic illness, which are as real as any others. So he'd have stomach ache, he'd have headaches and those things would increase. And then you'd get to the point where you think well you can't have that many stomach aches and headaches – go to school. Then something else would develop and it had to be more and more daring each time*

Teenagers may become school refusers for a number of reasons. It may be that they don't want to go to school, or it may be that they have reasons for wanting to stay at home.

> Reasons for wanting to avoid school include:
> - difficulties with school work or a particular teacher;
> - bullying;
> - isolation or difficulty in making friends;
> - anxiety about a particular activity such as PE.

> Reasons for wanting to stay at home include:
> - wanting (or needing) to care for an ill parent;
> - wanting to look after an abused sibling or parent;
> - wanting to monitor or sort out parental disagreement.

Helping a school refuser

There are a number of ways that parents can help a school refuser. Talk to your son or daughter, and let them know that you are concerned about them. Try to find out what the problem is, and talk about how you can help them to deal with it.

You should also consider discussing the problem with the school, especially if you find that your son or daughter is being bullied or is anxious about poor performance. They may well be able to help the teenager deal with the problem – perhaps by providing extra help with a difficult class, or changing teachers. Other problems the teenager is having may require the involvement of a professional, perhaps an educational psychologist. Your child's school will be able to put you in touch with one.

You may need to address the problems the teenager is having at home. If, for example, the problem is that the teenager is staying at home to look after you or a relative, then contacting social services to provide a home help may be an option.

It is important that teenagers who refuse to go to school are helped to deal with their problems as early as possible. Long-term absence from school means that your teenager will get out of the routine of attending, and make it all the more difficult for them to go back. In serious cases of school refusal, some local authorities have special schools (that are sometimes based in houses) available to encourage teenagers to attend and catch up on their education.

Truancy

Truanting teenagers often go to school and come home at the right time, but are absent from school in between.

Truanting teenagers:
- are often poor achievers;
- find school boring or irrelevant;
- feel the school or the teachers are not interested in them;
- have difficulty with authority or discipline;
- have a poor relationship with their parent(s);
- have a particular interest outside the school – in music or sport for example.

Parents of truants often don't know that their teenager is absent from school, only finding out by chance or when the school contacts them. It often comes as a considerable shock to a parent to find out that their teenager has been truanting from school.

Like school refusal, truancy must be dealt with, as many truants become part of a vicious cycle. Like school refusers, truants get behind at school, feel embarrassed and disaffected if they go back, and so start to truant again.

Again, if your teenager is truanting you need to find out why. It could be bullying, or fear of a particular teacher or subject. Other truants believe that school is of no relevance to them, and that it is boring or a waste of time. It is a good idea to contact the school and try to develop a plan of action with them. Getting a persistant truant to stay at school is not easy, but there are a number of strategies to try. These include focusing on the things that your teenager does find interesting or enjoyable at school – sport or music for example. The school may allow them to do extra sessions of these activities if they stay at school for the whole week. Some schools try to link staying at school with something that the teenager wants to do in the future – for example arranging a period of work experience in an area that interests them, and stressing that a certain number of exam passes are necessary to get into this work.

Teenagers with special needs

There are two groups of young people who may need special help whilst at school – gifted young people, and slow learners. We'll look at the needs of gifted teenagers first.

Gifted teenagers

Gifted teenagers usually stand out, as intellectually they are way ahead of their peers. Often a teenager will be particularly gifted in one area only (such as maths), although they may be gifted in all areas. Many will have taught themselves in a particular subject area.

Gifted teenagers can have problems at school. For example they may:

- be teased;
- get bored in class and muck about;
- be picked on or bullied;
- become withdrawn and have difficulty making friends.

There are a number of things that parents can do to help a gifted teenager:

- Find them some extra classes in subjects they're particularly interested in. If this proves to be expensive, try to find an interested or knowledgeable friend to help. Gifted teenagers need to feel they are being stretched.
- Find other outside activities that stimulate them and keep them interested – clubs, courses, libraries.
- Encourage them to be involved with friends of their own age. Many gifted children retire from their friends, or spend time with older teenagers. Gifted children may be advanced intellectually, but they need to develop socially and emotionally with other young people of their own age.

Learning difficulties

It is important to remember that teenagers with learning difficulties are quite different to teenagers with learning disabilities. Children and young people with a learning disability may, for example, have had a brain injury, and will have received special help throughout their educational career. Teenagers who have learning difficulties, on the other hand, may have dyslexia, or find learning difficult because of physical or emotional problems. They will normally attend mainstream schools, but may receive special help whilst at school.

A variety of help can be given to a teenager with a learning difficulty. In the school context these include:

- extra help with particular lessons;

- joining a class for young people with learning difficulties;
- transfer to a special school.

There is also much that parents can do to help a teenager who has a learning difficulty. You can:

- provide support and love – this may seem obvious, but teenagers need to know that despite their difficulties their parents love and value them;
- focus on the things that they can do well – for example art, sport or music;
- spend time alone with them going through their work. Practice with reading and writing can be particularly helpful. Be patient, and praise the progress they make.

This chapter has looked, fairly briefly, at some of the main aspects that affect young people's experience of education – homework, exams, part-time work, planning for the future, and special needs. Helping your teenager in many of these areas can be daunting, and you may be unsure where to get help and advice. The resources and organisations listed at the end of this chapter are a good place to start.

Further reading

A good book about education is *A parents' A-Z of education* by Hilary Mason and Tony Ramsey, Chambers, 1992.

The following book is a really useful guide to opportunities for young people, and includes information about volunteering, careers, sports and leisure, working holidays and hobbies. A copy has been placed in every main public library and secondary school: *Go for it*, by Martyn Lewis, Lennard, 1993.

A useful book on special needs is in the Headway Positive Parenting Series: *Your child with special needs* by Susan Kerr, Headway, Hodder & Stoughton, 1993.

A good book about children and teenagers with dyslexia is by Christine Ostler: *Dyslexia: A parents' survival guide*, Ammonite, 1991.

Useful organisations

The **Department for Education** can provide leaflets and information on all aspects of education. Contact the Department for Education, Sanctuary Buildings, Great Smith Street, Westminster, London, SW1P 3BT. Tel. 0171-925-5000.

Information, advice and support for parents and pupils in state schools is available from **ACE (Advice Centre for Education)**, 1B Aberdeen Studios, 22–24 Highbury Grove, London, N5 2EA. Tel. 0171-354-8321 (weekdays 2pm–5pm).

For information about education in Scotland, contact the **Scottish Education Department**, New Saint Andrew's House, Edinburgh, EH1 3SY. Tel. 0131-244-4445.

For the address of your local **Careers Service**, look up the Careers Office in the telephone directory, or look under Local Authority. There is an office in most towns and cities.

For information about social security, phone **Freeline Benefits Agency**. Tel. 0800-666555 (for England, Scotland and Wales), and 0800-616757 (for Northern Ireland).

Drive For Youth, based in the Snowdonia National Park, runs 22-week courses for long-term unemployed young people, helping to get them motivated, and trying to find jobs and training at the end. Free places are available. Contact Drive For Youth, Celmi Training Centre, Llanegryn, Nr Tywyn, Gwynedd, Wales, LL36 9SA. Or contact their London office: Drive For Youth, c/o Coopers and Lybrand, 32 Farringdon Street, London, EC4A 4AE. Tel. 0171-212-1563.

For information and advice about gifted children, contact the **National Association for Gifted Children**, Park Campus, Northampton, NN2 7AL. Tel. 01604-792300.

For information and advice about dyslexia contact the **British Dyslexia Association**, 98 London Road, Reading, RG1 5AU. Tel. 01734-668271.

CHAPTER NINE

From teenage to adulthood

This chapter reviews the main points we have made about building good relationships between parents and teenagers, and looks at the issue of teenagers becoming adults and parents letting go. It includes the following:

- Good communication
- Rules and boundaries
- Letting go and moving on

Good communication

In Chapters 1, 2 and 3, we looked at ways of developing good relationships between parents and teenagers. We showed that *communication* was central to this. It is essential to developing a good relationship with your teenager, and to having influence over them as they grow up.

Establishing good communication is not easy, however, as the comments from young people and their parents in this book have shown. Teenagers often say that parents 'just don't understand'. Parents say they 'can't get through' to their teenagers.

Communication can be improved. We suggested that the following dos and don'ts were essential to achieving this:

Don't
* make snap judgements;
* impose your ideas on teenagers;
* try to score points.

Do
* make time to listen;
* consider your teenager's point of view;
* show that you care about them;
* negotiate.

These things are not always easy to do of course. A fourteen-year-old wants to get a part-time job. A seventeen-year-old may be using drugs. A sixteen-year-old wants to stay out late at a friend's party. These can be difficult things to communicate about. Don't expect to have a good, open discussion every time you talk to your son or daughter! But it's important to persevere. Good communication does make a difference, but it has to be developed over time. And as we said early on, communication doesn't always have to involve talking. You and your teenager are communicating when you do an activity together, when you give each other a hug or a kiss. And of course you communicate with your teenager through your behaviour, as for example in how you deal with conflict, how you respond to setbacks, and so on.

Rules and boundaries

Good communication between parents and teenagers is essential for setting rules and boundaries with teenagers, and for making decisions with them. Teenagers must have – and will demand – an increasing say over their lives as they grow up.

A number of points that we made in earlier chapters about boundaries are worth re-stating here. In terms of establishing structure and rules, there are a variety of things that teenagers need:

- to have clear boundaries;
- to have a say in the rules that affect them;
- to have rules explained to them;
- to be monitored;
- to know there are penalties if the rules are broken.

In most cases decisions can, and should, be made jointly between parents and teenagers. Discussion, compromise and negotiation are central to effective decision-making. A number of guidelines can help the decision-making process:

- concentrate your efforts on the important issues;
- justify your viewpoint;
- stress that you care about your teenager;
- be consistent;
- be flexible; adapt rules to circumstances or events;
- give your teenagers increased responsibility as they get older.

Letting go and moving on

As we showed in Chapter 2, teenagers have an uncertain role in British society, and as a result there is no fixed point at which they become adults. Some cultures have a ceremony or single event which marks the move from adolescence to adulthood. In most Western societies, however, different young people achieve adult status at different times.

Teenagers need to be encouraged to see the transition to adulthood as a slow and gradual one. The things that we've talked about throughout this book should encourage this. These include:

- giving teenagers greater control over their lives as they get older;
- giving increased responsibility with age;
- reducing the number of rules and regulations over time;
- helping teenagers to make safe and sensible decisions about how they live their lives.

When teenagers become adults the relationship between parents and teenagers has to change. Adult children should ideally have a relationship with their parents that is more like close friends. This can, of course, be difficult. Parents are in a position of power and authority over children, and it can be hard to give that up, especially if you feel that your son or daughter is heading for trouble. At some point, however, young adults need to feel that they are making their own decisions, and if necessary, making their own mistakes.

Many of the parents we spoke to felt some anxiety about their son or daughter becoming an adult. Some talked about the loss of their main role of parent, about the fear of being alone, and of having to find a new focus in their lives. Others talked about their feelings that they were losing their child, and about their concerns about sending them out into the world.

Index